PLANT
THAT SPEAK,
SOULS
THAT SING

PLANTS
THAT SPEAK,
SOULS
THAT SING

Transform Your Life
With the Spirit of Plants

FAY JOHNSTONE

FINDHORN PRESS

Findhorn Press
One Park Street
Rochester, Vermont 05767
www.findhornpress.com

Text stock is SFI certified

Findhorn Press is a division of Inner Traditions International

Copyright © 2018 by Fay Johnstone

Disclaimer
The information in this book is given in good faith and is neither intended to diagnose any physical or mental condition nor to serve as a substitute for informed medical advice or care. Please contact your health professional for medical advice and treatment. Neither author nor publisher can be held liable by any person for any loss or damage whatsoever which may arise from the use of this book or any of the information therein.

A CIP record for this title is available from the Library of Congress

ISBN 978-1-84409-751-7 (print)
ISBN 978-1-84409-761-6 (e-book)

Printed and bound in the United States by Lake Book Manufacturing, Inc.
The text stock is SFI certified. The Sustainable Forestry Initiative® program promotes sustainable forest management.

10 9 8 7 6 5 4 3 2 1

Edited by Jacqui Lewis
Cover design by Richard Crookes
Text design and layout by Damian Keenan
This book was typeset in Adobe Garamond Pro, Calluna Sans, with ITC Century Std Book Condensed, and Trajan Pro used as display typefaces.

To send correspondence to the author of this book, mail a first-class letter to the author c/o Inner Traditions • Bear & Company, One Park Street, Rochester, VT 05767, and we will forward the communication, or contact the author directly at **www.fayjohnstone.com**

Contents

Introduction

Nature is a doorway that helps us awaken and feel alive. This book is an invitation for you to step through that doorway and encourage the wisdom and the beauty of the plant world into your life. In doing this, you will experience a more harmonious relationship with your true self and your environment and feel an altogether deeper sense of connection and wholeness.

I know I am not alone in needing connection with nature, loving plants and enjoying their company. For centuries gardeners have been talking to their plants and enjoying the results in beautiful blooming gardens, productive vegetable patches and a natural rhythm in tune with the earth's seasons and cycles. Connecting with plants is not a new idea; it's ancient, and yet it's more important now than ever. Many of us are reawakening to the call of nature, pining for the deep connection that is rooted in our origins. Whether it's through growing our own gardens, spending time in nature, learning about herbal medicine, turning to more natural products, an organic lifestyle or travelling to new landscapes, the song of the green world is calling out and touching us all.

I believe it begins with opening our eyes and hearts to the plants that are growing around us within our immediate environment. This connection does not have to be time-consuming or complicated; it can be made with a simple heartfelt smile of joy as you take in the beauty of a flower or the magnificence of a tree in full bloom. Of course, the more adventurous will enjoy the more complex meditation, plant ceremony, ritual and honouring featured in this book and those of you short on time might opt for the simpler exercises or look for more opportunities to spend time in nature. You are encouraged to start where you are comfortable.

It's time to make a conscious effort to schedule in walks in the rain, making angels in the snow, moon bathing, cloud watching and storytelling in the shade of the oak tree. Many barriers have sprung up, in our Western way of living, that separate us from nature. Not only do we spend the majority of our day behind closed doors or in front of a screen, but we think we run the world, rather than remembering that we are merely part of the whole organism. This book invites you to explore your relationship with plants by feeling rather than thinking and to expand your heart to a place of co-creation with nature, rather than from a mindset of dominion over nature. With the right mindset we can create the space for honouring nature and begin the process of remembering how plants do support us and how beautiful life can be when we work together.

It begins there in that moment when we consciously breathe; in that moment there is a connection with all that gives us life, all that gives us our breath. That breath from our plant friends, our breath of life.

Throughout this book I share many of the techniques that I developed during my years as a flower farmer in Nova Scotia and also, in the more urban years that have followed, from spending time with plants, gardening, making medicines, learning from others and teaching at workshops. These are my attempts to connect with plant consciousness, to bridge the gap between my life inside behind square walls and my nature self that lives and breathes with the green kingdom outside my window. Within these pages you won't find scientific facts and figures to persuade you of the benefits of interacting with plants. Instead, you will find an invitation to explore plants for yourself and experience the magic that happens when you take the time to feel your way.

My wish is for you to explore your nature connection, to guide you to see from your heart and not your head. May you breathe with the spirit of nature, may you reawaken your wild edges, may you merge into the nature that surrounds you to remember your own unique nature. May you open and be willing to experience plants as intelligent and ancient beings that have deep wisdom secrets to share with you.

Connecting to nature, and plants in particular, is not a one-off event; it's a lifelong journey of discovery that, I believe, can lead us to a healthier, more balanced world filled with love and abundance. Exploring nature more deeply is a journey to reclaim a lost language and rekindle a broken connection. This journey becomes an exploration into your own soul, as you reach in and touch the innermost parts of yourself. It all starts when we look out of the window and invite the green world in.

You may already have an inkling, a sense that there is much more to the plants that grow around you than you have been led to believe; this book will help you follow your senses, develop an understanding and feel your way with your heart. The book's exercises will expand your consciousness to help you experience plants in a new way while at the same time providing you with support for your journey of plant discovery and permission to play.

There are many exercises throughout this book, but don't feel you have to rigidly stick to following each one – make space for your intuition and the plants to guide you. If you don't feel that a particular exercise is appropriate for you then please honour your feelings and simply don't do that one. You can always revisit it later or with a different plant. Likewise if an exercise is suggesting one thing and your body, mind and soul are screaming out to do something else then please go ahead and follow what you need to do.

My suggestions are guidelines and as you follow them the exercises will shift and expand into something else as your energy interacts with plant consciousness and the exercise becomes part of something bigger than you or I could have imagined. Don't be afraid to go with the flow and honour the magic of the moment. Dance, cry, laugh, cook, paint, write, bury your hands in the earth, hug a tree – do what you need to do, as spirit moves you and moves through you. If you find yourself engrossed in the exercises and wanting more, then simply explore different plants and go deeper. Every action from the heart will bring you closer to the realm and the complex language of nature and her plant spirits.

Start where you are – if all you can do is bring a pot plant inside or care for the neglected plants in your office building, then do just that. Start a journal for your plant adventures and note all your experiences; these may be feelings, poetry, drawings, colour, plant pressings, recipe notes, plant stories, insight, memories, dreams… Keep it simple, make it fun, honour your feelings, stay open and curious and let the green kingdom nourish your heart and soul.

PART ONE

REDISCOVERING
YOUR NATURE SELF

My Story: How I Woke Up
to the Spirit of Plants

"If the sight of the blue skies fills you with joy,
if a blade of grass springing up in the fields
has power to move you, if the simple things of nature
have a message that you understand,
rejoice, for your soul is alive."

— ELEONORA DUSE, Actress

Like many of us who were lucky enough to grow up outside of a city, I can proudly boast childhood memories of racing around the garden barefoot on summer days, climbing trees, crawling in and out of hedges and not giving a second thought to communing with fairies at the bottom of the garden. As I grew older, though, the lure and responsibility of the adult world took hold and adventures in nature were no longer on the daily agenda. There was no space for plant interaction, no room for my nature self. This nature-friendly part of me became sidelined, reserved for weekends only, something that I would only experience on weekend countryside walks that usually ended in a pub, or mini-breaks away to paddle in the sea. I became infected with the travel bug and the landscapes and culture of far-flung foreign lands seemed to have more appeal than the beauty and tradition that was close to home.

As if an invisible boundary had been placed in my way, I had become disconnected from nature. My relationship with nature had become distant and uncertain – in fact, my entire relationship with my wild and magical self had drifted far away. It took me a while to admit just how depressed I had become, being trapped in an office all day with only my lunch hour to take a walk and breathe some air. Something had to change.

Moving out of the city was a step forward that I was fortunate enough to be able to take. From a small commuter town in Hertfordshire I began a re-wilding or remembering process by taking walks in nature, enjoying my small garden, growing my own vegetables, wild harvesting, creating herbal potions and bringing plants inside my home. I even started a BSc in herbal medicine, such was my enthusiasm for plants and herbs.

My partner and I both nurtured a dream to live somewhere with space to play, grow and live with the land. We immersed ourselves in a quest for an affordable property, searching from France to the Scottish Highlands and across the Atlantic. In 2009, following a chance encounter with a couple who were selling a 35-acre farmstead in Nova Scotia, Canada, we found ourselves facing a decision: were we prepared to follow our dream or not? Well, as it turns out we were and in the spring of the following year we took the leap and moved to the farmstead. Looking back, we never really had a concrete plan, but soon after landing we set up an organic flower and herb farm. It was when all the growing took off and we had plants sprouting in all directions that I really began to acknowledge my connection to nature consciousness and plants in particular.

For five years my partner and I danced nature's song in flowers and herbs, braving the bugs and the long, freezing winters. It was here, immersed in the beauty of flowers and plants of all shapes and sizes, that an awareness of something so much larger than me was rekindled. An awakening to nature consciousness, to the plant spirits, to the elements; a deep remembering had begun. Spending so much time outside connected to the earth, working with plants in tune with the seasons – spending more time with plants than people in fact – I suppose a conscious relationship with plants was inevitable. It crept up on me, like some friendships do, and opened my heart in a gentle but insistent way. An irreversible process really, the start of a journey and a real gift. It was an experience that took me far beyond all the herbal medicine books, gardening magazines and plant guides that I had consumed for years. An experience that took me wonderfully out of my head and into my heart. I would best describe it as a deep unfolding of wisdom, a wide opening that recreated a long-forgotten bond of conspiracy and companionship.

I started experiencing the plants around me as people, with different personalities and preferences. Plants would appear to me as I was sleeping, or sitting having a cup of tea, with a message that something needed doing in the field. As soon as I woke in the morning and glanced out of the window, a kind of knowing would surround me, always with a sense of urgency! This intense immersion and interaction with the plant world in this way led me to develop a holistic view of plant medicine, far deeper and more personal than any of the herbals and gardening books that I had read over the years. I was guided to create essences and herbal medicines, as well as lovely floral arrangements that brought great joy to my clients. Up until this point I had only thought to use plants by making a physical medicine, like a herbal tincture, flower essence, infused oil or homeopathic remedy. However, the invisible essence or spirit of plants was now appearing to me so strongly that I began to realize that the real transformational power of the plant lies in connecting to its spirit or vital force. I started using plants with my clients in one-to-one reiki treatments. I would notice that before a client arrived, particular plants would be desperately seeking my attention and I simply knew that they had healing to share with the client. The alchemical nature of plants and their ability to transform us not only on a physical level but also on an emotional and spiritual level became very clear to me and was noticed by my clients too.

Thanks to the plants my consciousness expanded to meet their wisdom. I was gifted with poetry, song, dance, medicine, understanding and a heart so full that it sat wide open in my chest full of joy. The plants had unlocked something inside of me, a part of me that had become buried and constrained by a sense of obligation and duty. Somehow, through my connections with the plants, they had reached in and found the real me. It was as if they could see my truth, even though I hadn't a clue about it! I changed, I mellowed, I laughed more and wasn't so angry. I was held by these green beings, all of me, and it was OK.

This partnership became so much a natural part of me and my new sense of being in the world that I didn't realize how unusual it was. I only felt the depth of that connection as a sense of heavy loss when I was no longer living at the farm, no longer attached to the plants but on the other side of the Atlantic once again.

My partner and I had felt the pull of our heartstrings and decided to leave our farm and return to the UK, leaving beautiful plants and an invisible connection that I had learned to love and was so comfortable to be surrounded by.

I began the process of plugging myself back in again, re-attuning to my new environment in the Scottish Borders. It was a struggle but I was determined to keep the magic of my nature self alive inside and maintain the relationship with plant consciousness that I had rekindled in Nova Scotia. How could I maintain my connection with plants in this way and yet function wholeheartedly in this new environment that was more urbanized and populated? I had forgotten just how cut off from nature our towns and cities can be. It was far too easy to be lured back into a life predominantly spent inside. I hadn't had a mobile phone for five years and wow… well, you know all about that distraction!

What I experienced in Nova Scotia was such a gift and I am on a quest to connect people, like you, with plants to experience a similar transformation and expansion of consciousness. How can we bridge the gap between our Western routines and urban living, with all its modern conveniences, and nature consciousness? How can we at the same time connect with nature and honour the role that it plays in feeding our souls and making our hearts come alive with song? We are not all going to flee the cities, hunker down to rural life and get back to the land. We like our home comforts far too much. But I know there is a space in me – in all of us – for our nature connection. The space of permission, the space of honouring and acknowledging, the space of discovery and healing. The space of remembering and reforging bonds that have been long neglected.

I began to run workshops sharing techniques and simply holding the space for participants to spend time with plants and connect with them. What I noticed most of all was that these workshops were the permission people needed to come, relax and connect. Participants needed the space to simply be in the gardens, connect in the green silence of nature and invite the magic in. That space starts for you with this book.

Questions for Self-reflection

1. How has the role of nature and plants in your life changed since your childhood?
2. Do you spend as much time with nature as you would like?
3. How might your life be different if you did spend more time with nature?
4. How can you make space in your life to include more nature, to honour your nature self and to acknowledge your connection?

Over the next few chapters, join me on a journey to discover what lies in your heart space and feel your way into your rhythm within the natural cycle of all things.

Heart Space: Know Yourself and Your Plant Story

"I only went out for a walk and finally concluded to stay out till sundown, for going out, I found, was really going in."

— JOHN MUIR, author and naturalist

EXERCISE **The Call of the Wild (and the Urban Park)**

Put down this book and go outside. Find a patch of grass (preferably in the sun) and kick off your shoes.

There! Now you have landed, now you can connect, now you can remember.

Initially the grass may feel cold to your feet but you will be surprised how quickly you'll get used to it. By the end of this short exercise you will find yourself reluctant to put your shoes back on.

So just be for a moment in this space, with your bare feet touching the soft grass beneath you.

Let your arms hang down, close your eyes and take in three deep breaths here in this moment.

Now become aware once again of those feet.

Imagine roots growing out of the soles of your feet and growing through the soil deep down into the earth. Imagine these roots travelling through the layers of the soil, past the fossils, rocks, precious stones, decomposing and decaying matter, travelling right down, deep down into the heart of the earth.

Imagine at this heart of the earth a warm fire bursting with creativity, passion, love and care. Allow your roots to feel warmed by this fire and bring that warmth up through the layers of the soil back into your feet.

Now that you are firmly rooted here, bring your awareness to the space that surrounds you.

What can you hear?

Can you feel the wind on your skin?

The sun?

Any dampness?

Are there any fragrances in the air?

Is there a feeling in the air today?

Place your hands on your heart and focus your breathing into this area, as if you are breathing in and out through your heart.

Breathe in the sounds that you hear, breathe them into your heart and allow them to fill your body. Breathe out gratitude.

Breathe in the wind that touches your skin, allow it right into your heart and throughout your entire body. Breathe out gratitude.

Breathe in the sun that warms your skin and allow it right into your heart and throughout your entire body. Breathe out gratitude.

Breathe in the dampness that cools your skin and allow it right into your heart and throughout your entire body. Breathe out gratitude.

Breathe in any fragrances or odours that are surrounding you, breathe these right into your heart and throughout your entire body. Breathe out gratitude.

If there is anything else that you sense, continue breathing these parts in and allowing your heart to open a little more each time, opening up your entire body to the sensations that are surrounding you.

Open out your arms as wide as you dare and be in this moment, open and exposed to the elements, open and inviting to the nature that surrounds you. Breathe here.

Feel this connection running through your body, your heart and your soul.

Allow it to awaken those hidden shadow parts of you that have long been forgotten.

Ask for the blessings of nature.

Bring your fingers to cover your eyes – asking to see truth.

Then to your throat – asking to speak truth.

Then to your ears – asking to hear truth.

Then to your heart – asking to feel your truth.

Be still here for a few minutes and listen.

Bring your attention back to your feet for a moment, recognize those roots that attach you always to Mother Earth, give thanks for the nourishment, support and warmth that you receive unconditionally from the earth.

Give thanks for this moment and any guidance you have received, open your eyes and release your hands from your heart.

Be outside for as long as you feel necessary. Notice what you are drawn to and how you are feeling.

Write down everything in your journal – the simplest of things, easily forgotten, often carry the most power.

Know Your Heart

Before you begin the exciting journey of remembering your connection with plants and expanding your consciousness to communicate with them, it helps to be really clear on your starting point. What I'm referring to is a clear understanding and awareness of yourself, your truth and your current challenges, together with an awareness of your current relationship with plants and the nature around you where you live.

How often do you allow yourself time to pause to consider your personal growth, desires or purpose in life?

Do you take notice of the plants that grow in your vicinity?

I refer to this space of inner knowing and authenticity as our heart space, as opposed to our head space, the space in which we are most used to spending time. When we are able to draw our perception down into our heart space and experience the world through our heart, this is where the magic happens. I find that when I am operating from my heart space my perception becomes more intuitive, less logical and calculated, softer and more open.

Consider your heart as a key organ of perception, a unique kind of brain. Your heart is both a cognitive and a perceptual organ, and has an electromagnetic field that radiates two and a half to three metres beyond your body, which makes it a powerful electromagnetic generator and receiver.

What you will perceive when you start living from the heart is quite different from what you perceive when you live in the head. You will already have a sense of what the heart field feels like. It's that feeling of being in someone's personal space when you are standing too close, say 30–45 cm away. You can practise feeling into this heart field with a friend: start about two metres apart and walk slowly towards each other. At a certain point you will begin to feel that you are in their space. This is your two heart fields touching. Practise getting to know the feel of your heart field so that you can use it as an extension of your senses to touch and feel the world around you. Herbalist and teacher Stephen Harrod Buhner has written extensively on the heart as our primary organ of perception (visit the bibliography to discover his work).

For all of the exercises in this book and when you're spending time with plants, practise exploring the world from your heart space. Practise being present to what your heart is picking up on and transmitting. Leave your judgement and critic aside and explore in a childlike way, with compassion and curiosity.

Being in a state of joy and gratitude carries an electromagnetic vibration that is highly attractive and magnetic. Bear this is mind when beginning your relationships with plants – an attitude of gratitude and appreciation is going to make it easier for plants to be attracted to your vibration and respond to you.

Think about people you know and what vibration they carry. Consider someone who is shy and fearful as opposed to someone who is full of life; think beyond how they behave and feel into the vibration that they carry and notice the difference.

Consider the last time you experienced someone being angry or were with someone who was filled with sadness; again feel into the vibration that these emotions carry and start to recognize it.

Think about someone who you met recently who you didn't really get on with, or think back to dates you have been on – sometimes people say all the right things and behave in all the right ways but you just don't click. Learn to recognize when things do work with your vibration and when they don't.

What vibration do you think you carry? Can you change this to suit your mood? Consider your actions: do you think that some of your actions carry different vibrations than others? Would, for example, an act of kindness vibrate at the same level as malicious gossip?

Experiment with friends, family and colleagues. Open yourself up to these subtle energies and see if you can sense into people's presence when you are with them. This is much easier with people you already know because you will already be attuned to their energy on some level and familiar with it, even though you might not be 100% conscious of that yet.

Remember that you can choose to change your vibration. If you are having a bad day that isn't flowing well, find a plant that looks like it is thriving. Spend ten minutes breathing with that plant and place it in your heart. You are bound to feel better afterwards.

EXERCISE Heart Space Connection

Sit comfortably with your eyes closed in a space where you are not going to be disturbed and start focusing on the breath leaving and entering your body.

Simply breathe deeply right into the centre of your being and exhale as far out as you can before beginning again.

Try to take long, calming breaths, allowing yourself to relax a little more with each exhalation.

Place your hands on your heart centre. Lower your attention from your head into your heart.

Keep breathing and visualize each breath entering and leaving from your heart as you breathe out and in.

Maintain your focus on your breath and on your hands to keep your attention on your heart space. Imagine your heart opening a little more and filling up with each breath that you take.

Bring to mind a joyful experience or someone you love and allow your heart to expand into that joy, as if you were radiating the vibration of joy out from your heart. Feel this vibration of joy travelling out of your heart, throughout your entire body and into the energy field around you.

Stay centred here, radiating joy for as long as you feel comfortable, then release your hands, open your eyes and end the practice.

You can also access this at: **www.plantsthatspeak.com.**

How does it feel to be in that space? What feeling or sensation does it stir in you? Now, from your heart space, consider the following personal goals:

- What's the biggest challenge in your life right now?
- Do you consider yourself content or are you still striving for something?
- What brings you joy and makes your heart sing?
- Why are you really reading this book? What are you secretly hoping for?

Developing Self-awareness and Compassion through Meditation

Developing a sense of self-awareness, the ability to really listen and hear with an open heart, and being mindfully present are key to successful relationships (and not just with the plant world!). Being aware of our emotions and opening up our sensual awareness in our bodies through our senses are key tools to assist us in meeting the essential nature of plants. Often when I am working with plants I might feel a sensation in my body, like intense heat, or often my ears pop like crazy and the pressure changes. It helps to know what's normal for me so I can more easily recognize any sensations that are unusual and different and may be caused by a plant.

Regular meditation or mindfulness practice and mindful movement practices like yoga or Five Rhythms dance can help with this. There are so many apps available now and meditation teachers around. Personally I have found that having a regular meditation practice is essential for maintaining my sanity in today's world of total overwhelm, not to mention that it is a big help for a journey on any spiritual path.

Try the following one-minute meditation to centre yourself at any moment of the day, whenever you feel the need.

MEDITATION Five Calming Breaths

Sit comfortably with your eyes closed in a space where you are not going to be disturbed, breathe normally and start focusing on your breath.

Simply breathe deeply, right into the centre of your being, and exhale as far out as you can before beginning again.

Focus your attention onto the journey of the breath, following it right down into your body and all the way out as you exhale.

Allow your shoulders to drop and feel your body relax a little more each time you exhale.

- When you have taken a few breaths to still yourself, breathe in deeply again and as you finish exhaling your first breath, say the following short mantra to yourself: 'I begin.'
- Breathe in and exhale again and this time say 'I let go.'
- Breathe in and exhale a third time and this time say 'I calm.'
- Breathe in and exhale a fourth time and this time say 'I connect.'
- Breathe in and exhale a final time and as you release this time say 'I shine.'

You can carry on for as long as you need to feel calm and centred. If you find that you don't need the mantras then either don't use words at all or replace them with others.

You can also access this meditation at: **www.plantsthatspeak.com.**

Healing Broken Hearts and
Finding Lost Magic in Nature

For the past fifteen years, since I have been a practitioner of reiki and more recently in my shamanic practice, I have treated many clients suffering from stress or depression. Often during the course of a series of treatments it becomes clear that the client, for whatever reason, has forgotten their magic and become disconnected from their heart, their wonderful unique essence and their true self. In shamanism this is often referred to as soul loss and it is when, due to the trauma of life events, the soul – our unique self – has become fragmented and parts of it have disconnected from the whole or become hidden.

Many of us go to immense lengths to discover our passion and soul purpose, searching for a life with meaning and value. We can get so lost and frustrated, desperate to be or to achieve something, but we are often very far away from getting in touch with what that magical something is because we are disconnected from our sense of wholeness. Yet I've never met a sapling that did not know what kind of tree it was to grow into. I've never met a seedling that did not know what type of flower it was to be (and what colour). Nature knows. Since we are nature, then so do we. In my experience nature is a powerful healer in terms of aligning us with our true essence and helping restore wholeness to our soul. Once we open up to nature, we gain a much deeper sense of life and our place in the cosmic web. Plants help us feel more whole and integrated into life; they help us remember who we are so we can fulfil our purpose here on earth. I believe that the plant world can help us raise our consciousness and live a more fulfilling life in harmony with the earth, being fully ourselves.

Our lives have become urbanized, sanitized and vacuum-packed, far removed from the nature-paced lifestyle of our ancestors. To rediscover our nature self, we need to reweave the green thread into our lives, bring down the invisible divide that has been erected between us and the nature that lies outside of us. I don't think we meant to put it up there dividing us from our Mother, but over time it has become such a vast obstacle and, particularly when I am working with clients suffering from depression, it is one of the first things that has to come down. A simple daily walk in nature is a good place to start, together with a healthy habit of turning off all devices so you can experience stillness.

What do you do to access the stillness in your heart and clear your head? What is the source of your health?

Exploring Your Personal Plant Story

There is a part within all of us that feels at home in nature. Neuroscience reveals that our brains behave differently in nature and that time in nature relieves stress and helps us not only feel better but also think better.

The common thread that runs through all the participants on my workshops is that they have always felt a connection with plants, since they were young children. Like myself in my city days, each participant, through no deliberate action, has somehow lost that connection with plants and nature and feels that loss deeply. For some it's a nostalgia for childhood or the loss of a loved one, for others it's the call of the wild and the wildness within them and for others again it's a desire to interact more deeply with their gardens and special places in nature. Many people are also incredibly sensitive to the devastation and damage that we humans are inflicting on the earth. For most people, more often than not it's a feeling that the plants around them are carrying a message and have a definite purpose, which can no longer be ignored and calls to be discovered and heard.

I am very aware of how the role of plants in my life has changed over time and how certain trees or plants have left a strong impression that has shaped my attachment to them. As a child I loved playing around the trees in our garden. I have particularly fond memories of an enormous ornamental cherry tree and its beautiful May blossom. My friends and I would make crowns of blossom and wear them until they simply flopped off us onto the ground. I buried both of my hamsters under that tree and spent many happy days playing beneath the branches. Myself and my neighbour played for years in a huge horse chestnut tree in her front yard. Countless hours were spent up there laughing, playing, plotting and growing. We used to play games of conkers with the shiny brown seeds and spike ourselves with the green thorny seed pods.

Then one day my neighbour fell from the tree and was rushed to hospital and our days with this tree came to an end. It saddened me greatly. We then both grew up and moved on, but I always felt so safe and protected by this tree that I still retain much nostalgia for the horse chestnut; it feels like a representation of my childhood innocence – now lost, of course!

The apple trees at the bottom of the garden were another refuge in which to hide away and play. My dad had attached a rope ladder to one, which would rock the whole tree as you climbed, making apples fall from it. The apple tree was friendly and safe but the apples were tart and sour.

A giant cypress, however, was my true hiding place. I used to pull down one of her branches and enter into the tree like it was a cave. The branch would swing up and close behind me, enveloping me in the centre of the tree branches. I would always emerge faintly scented and with twigs in my hair. This is where I learnt the secrets of cypress and this memory is part of her medicine for me.

My childhood is also filled with memories of buddleia at the bottom of the garden, soft, scented garden mints and the pretty, delicate daisy chains we would all make on the school playing field.

Hawthorn

Growing up in a small village in the English countryside, I was surrounded by this ancient plant. Hawthorn hedgerows lined the roadsides and divided our property from the neighbours. Of course, being children we would always find a hole in the hedge and use it to crawl through into the unknown. I still remember the scratchy feel of hawthorn's thorns scraping my hands, legs and back as I crawled through countless hedges.

We would often find birds' nests, insects, mice and sweet-smelling honeysuckle. Now my relationship with hawthorn has matured (only slightly!) and rather than crawl, I prefer to lay myself down at her feet. I look forward to the delicate bloom each May and the rich berries each autumn. There is such a sense of fairy energy about this plant, I can get lost in its magic and medicine.

Hawthorn, I open my heart to you.

Obviously not all plant memories are fond ones. Many of us will have experienced the discomfort of poison ivy or stinging nettles as adventurous (foolish?) children or the harsh prickles of roses, thistles and brambles. Jamie, my partner, will never forget his first memory of a chilli plant. Exploring with his curious fingers was great fun, until the part where he unthinkingly rubbed his eyes... ouch! Some relationships just don't get off to a great start.

Questions for Self-reflection

Sit yourself down in a quiet space with no interruptions, try the previous Five Calming Breaths meditation to centre yourself and consider the following. If nothing comes to you immediately, no problem – sit with the question for a few days and see what comes.

1. Cast your mind back to your childhood. What is your earliest memory of plants? Note down the plants that have had an impact on your life.
2. Did you as a child have a favourite place in nature? How did it make you feel?
3. Today, are there any plants – flowers, herbs, trees or simply places in nature – that you feel drawn to? Or choose to avoid? Ask yourself why.
4. How do these plants or places make you feel? Include positive feelings as well as negative. Sense into your body and ask yourself where do you feel those feelings? Your head, heart, throat, belly? How do you sense this? What sensations occur in your body? Tingling, heat or cold, or a tightness, or anything else?
5. When was the last time you felt touched by nature? How did you sense that connection? Where did you feel it in your body?
6. Do you remember the first time you gave or were given flowers? What feelings do you recall?
7. Has a plant or a place in nature deeply touched your life? How?

MEDITATION Experience Yourself as a Garden

Find a space where you are not going to be disturbed, sit or lie comfortably with your eyes closed and start focusing on your breath. Simply breathe deeply right into the centre of your being and exhale as far out as you can before beginning again.

Focus your attention on the journey of the breath, following it right down into your body and all the way out again as you exhale.

Allow your shoulders to soften and feel your body relax a little more each time you exhale.

In your mind's eye envisage a place in nature that you know well. Take a good look around you, really absorbing the colours and the sounds of your surroundings.

See a staircase appear in front of you, with ten steps leading down. At the bottom of these stairs is a gate to your inner garden.

Begin to descend slowly, one step at a time, and with each step down towards your garden leave your ordinary reality behind.

At the bottom of the steps, open the gate and enter the garden. Here is your personal garden, where you can grow, rest, blossom and mix with other plants and wildlife.

Walk slowly around your garden; notice how it appears. Do the plants look healthy and strong? Bend down and touch the soil. Is it dry or damp? Does it seem fertile? Does it need anything?

Is grass growing in your garden, or are there rocks? Is your garden wild or very well maintained? Does it look like someone looks after it in any way? Are there any areas that look like they need more attention and care?

Take yourself to an area where new seeds have been planted. What are these seeds? What do they need to help them grow?

Can you see anything growing in your garden that you no longer wish to have there? Is there anything that it no longer serves you to maintain? What can you pull up, chop down or cut back? Perhaps there is something that is overcrowding another plant? Make sure that everything that you wish to grow has the space and the water that it needs to be healthy and vibrant.

Take a seat in your garden to appreciate its beauty and breathe in the vibrant energy of the powerful plants that grow there and surround you. Feel into your heart and allow yourself a sense of excitement at the potential of what is growing. Match your heartbeat to the beat of your garden.

This is your garden: you are the caretaker, the gardener and the designer. Are you feeding your garden with love and care?

Connect into the earth, sending invisible roots down from your feet into the ground. Send those roots right down into the heart of the earth, through its many layers. Reach the heart of Mother Earth, the creative fire at the centre, and send your roots into this centre to receive nourishment and energy from the heart of the earth. Send this nourishment and energy up through your roots, through the many layers of the earth, back into your feet and up and around your entire body. Send each cell in your body the nourishment and healing energy of the earth. Silently give thanks.

When you are ready, leave your garden from the same point that you entered, knowing that you can come back here whenever you need to.

Climb back up the steps and with each step you take, leave your garden experience behind you and bring yourself back to your normal life.

When you reach the top of the steps, start to become aware of your body, feeling the weight of your body on the floor beneath you. Wriggle your fingers and toes, wrists and ankles to bring movement back. Place your palms over your eyes and open your eyes behind them.

When you feel ready, remove your hands and, if you were lying down, move into a seated position. Breathe here, relaxing for as long as you need. Make notes in your journal for reflection.

Take a drink of water and make sure you feel fully grounded and awake before resuming your day.

You can also access this meditation at: **www.plantsthatspeak.com**.

Chapter Summary

The ideas in this beginning chapter are to help you create and cultivate a healthy awareness of your sacred heart space, your wishes, desires, feelings and intentions. Your heart space is a familiar centre point for you to begin from and come back to as you venture into relationships with plants and the natural world around you over the course of the following chapters.

KEY POINTS

- Experience your heart space through stillness, meditation and daily journaling.
- Practise spending time viewing life through your heart space, rather than your head space.
- Know your heart, what brings it joy, what it needs to sing.
- Explore your personal plant stories and the role that plants already play in your life.

In the next chapter you are invited to explore your environment, find your rhythm, honour the moon and flow with the cycles of the seasons. This will help you begin to know and become rooted in where you are, what's going on in your life and how that affects your feelings and behaviour and, most importantly, how you fit in with and are influenced by the natural world around you.

Feel Rooted: Find Your Rhythm

"Come forth into the light of things,
Let Nature be your teacher…
…Come forth, and bring with you a heart
That watches and receives."

— **WILLIAM WORDSWORTH**, from the poem "The Tables Turned"

In my experience, the more time I spend hanging out with plants and taking notice of the natural cycles of the year, the more in tune I am with my very own nature, the part of me that knows my truth, my intuition and wisdom of ages. This was easy to do when we ran the farm because the growing season was at the mercy of the weather and the seasons and therefore so was I.

For many years I used to loathe the coming of winter and the dreary winter months with their short days and damp chill in the air. How I longed for summer! This feeling has taken some beating but now, as those first autumn leaves begin to fall I no longer experience a dread of the winter that is to come. I gladly let go of the busyness of the summer months and it comes as a comfort to know that the nights will get longer and the pace will slow; it means that I can take refuge.

When we let go of the illusion that we have to live at full pace all of the time, perform at our peak, always blossoming or firing all cylinders, and accept that like the seasons of the year we too can have our cycles, we can begin a much more authentic flow that resonates with our soul and our time of life.

Imagine how exhausting it would be for a beautiful cherry tree to be in blossom all year. It simply would not be able to sustain such a performance and, if it was so constant, would we even appreciate its beauty?

Questions for Self-reflection

1. Are there areas in your life where you are trying to always be at the top of your game? What are they?

2. Think of your life in terms of the seasons of the year. In which areas of your life are you in spring? What is new that is emerging?
3. In which areas of your life are you in summer? What is blooming for you?
4. In which areas of your life are you in autumn? What projects are you reaping the benefits of now? What habits and attitudes no longer serve you and are ready to be dropped like a tree drops its · leaves?
5. In which areas of your life are you in winter? Where are you at rest, creating projects and plans for the spring?

Developing Your Relationship with Nature at Home

In my experience getting a feel for a place takes time. Time spent hanging out, absorbing the energy of the place, time spent wandering the streets and pathways, time spent seeking out the places where you feel safe and powerful, time spent seeking out the beauty and the stillness. Fortunately for me, I am a dog owner, which means that daily I have a reason to get up and out of the door. Rain or shine, I have the opportunity to tread a new path or enjoy a familiar trail. In doing these twice-daily walks with my dog I have got to know the place where I now live. It didn't happen overnight but my feel for the place, the spirit of it, has sunk in over time. I now know where to forage for elderberries, blackberries and raspberries. I now know which places to avoid at certain busy times and I have my favourite places to go on sunny days or clear starry evenings.

Start opening up your senses to the seasons of the year and how they affect your local area and how you feel about it. Go beyond the obvious and feel into the energy and the feeling that characterizes each season and what effect they have on you and your surroundings. If you find this difficult, try remembering how you were as a child and what you would have explored or been drawn to. Keep an eye out for local festivals; these traditional fetes and village celebrations may reveal a lot about the energy of a specific time of year.

Each year at my primary school, not only did we have to learn how to dance round the maypole in the village for the annual May Day celebrations on 1 May (this meant we had to hold hands with boys, which was horrifying!), but there was also a tradition to vote for a May Queen from our peers at school. As luck would have it, one sunny May it turned out to be my year; I was given the honour of being the May Queen. From what I remember, this consisted of wearing a crown of flowers on my head and a pretty dress and being carried around school all day. I still remember the sense of privilege, the feeling of fun, the laughter and the wonderful cherry blossom that was out in our garden at that time of year. This experience has most definitely contributed to May being my favourite time of the year and my feeling that all good things begin in May!

Questions for Self-reflection

1. How do you feel about where you live? Is there a certain energy in your area that is different to the surrounding areas?
   What qualities does the land hold? What personality does it have? Is it full of sadness? Joy? Other feelings?
2. Where do you feel at peace? Do you have a favourite place?
3. How well do you know the area and the community? Do you know where the sun rises and sets, where the moon rises in the sky and what phase it is in? Where the wind comes from in summer? In winter?
4. What parts of where you live resonate with you? If nothing about where you live does, then imagine or remember where you have been that does. Write down the qualities and features that resonate with you.
5. How do you interact with the nature around you? Perhaps you have a garden that you enjoy, or a small balcony or terrace? Perhaps you go for a daily run, or dog-walk?
6. How well do you know the trees and plants where you live? Do you have any favourites? How often do you visit them?
7. Do you have a favourite time of day? Does this change depending on the time of year?
8. What is your favourite time of year and why?
9. Where do you feel most grounded and rooted?
10. Where in you lives your wildness?

Cycling with the Moon and the Earth

A moon cycle occurs every 29½ days or so and begins on the new moon and journeys through the different phases, waxing through full moon and waning back to the new moon again. You can get free apps that track the moon cycle (if you are unable to look up into the sky on a clear night).

Following the cycle of the moon provides a natural rhythm to help you stay awake to and active in the creative process of your life. The time around the new moon is perfect for introspection, so take the time to pause, acknowledge what has passed in the previous cycle and consider what you wish to manifest and focus on for the cycle to come. Beginning each moon cycle with a potent intention for what you want to call into your life, or giving the moon cycle a particular theme, is a powerful practice. As you work more closely with plants and the moon cycles you may find that for each cycle a plant calls to you and offers to be your guide or support for a particular cycle.

As the moon waxes and wanes, explore the intention that you have set for the cycle and dance with it. What is it going to take to bring this to life? Spend time with the plant that you are working with for this moon cycle and consider how this plant can help you. What qualities does the plant have that you can bring to your dance for this cycle?

If at first you don't feel particularly drawn to working with specific plants, simply cannot choose or don't know where to start, consider the Celtic tree calendar. In this calendar there are 13 months, each of which follows the different cycles of the moon and corresponds to a different tree. See what resonates with you and what you have available to you in your area.

Note your feelings at different stages of the moon cycle and over time check to see if there is a pattern that recurs. Don't assume that there is a certain way to feel at a particular stage of the moon cycle; we are all different animals with different experiences and we all react differently. My advice is not to read too much but be your own guide; go play and experience.

Do you ever spend time in the moonlight? Whenever you get the opportunity, go for a walk or stand and bathe under the light of the full moon. Allow its light to soak into your being and welcome the magic from the night sky into your heart.

The concept of cycles does not just apply to the moon; each day is part of a shorter cycle as the sun comes up, reaches a peak high in the sky (around midday) and then goes down. Notice what time of day your energy feels at its highest. Are you a morning person or a night owl? Start using the flow of your energy throughout the day to your benefit. Know when you need to rest and plan activities or meetings for when you know your energy will be at its most vibrant.

Sacred Space

To help me remain balanced and fully present to my life and inner guidance, I not only cultivate an inner sacred space, through my meditation practice, but I also maintain a physical space that is sacred to me. This doesn't mean that I am always off visiting historic sites, temples or ancient forests. Sacred space can be created in your home or workplace for daily reflection, connection and renewal.

What Does Sacred Space Mean to You?

You may find that images of large cathedrals, Buddhist temples, elaborate mosques and other symbols of religious worship come to mind. Consider more widely what is sacred for you. I find that when I am out in nature and allow myself to open up to the beauty around me, I can feel a divine presence in nature, without reference to specific doctrines or traditions.

Certain places on the earth are special to us; they help lift our spirits when we are down and restore harmony. You may find that as your sense of awareness grows and as you open up further to your relationship with nature consciousness, sacred spaces in nature reveal themselves. They have a habit of growing on us. Find a sacred earth place that energizes you and make sure that you schedule in time to go there.

Why Do We Need Sacred Space?

A sacred space is a place in which you can seek retreat, connect with and contemplate life's mystery and challenges. In sacred space, you can ask questions, reflect on your personal life experience, perform ritual, celebrate, sing, dance, invoke magic, journey to meet spirit guides, search for meaning, meditate, read poetry and listen to silence, all in the attempt to seek answers and guidance. You can reconnect with your sense of self, remember your qualities and achievements, honour where you are now, strengthen your intentions and envision your dreams.

Creating a sacred space is not obligatory for communicating with the natural world but I highly recommend it anyway, as a way to nourish your dreams and find balance. By allocating an area in your home as a sacred space, you create for yourself a place for quiet reflection, like a centre point that is separate from all of the business of your normal day. Here in your sacred space you can honour whatever you like. If you have a garden, then you may choose to create an external sacred space to help you connect and tune in to the plants that surround you.

EXERCISE **Create a Sacred Space**

This exercise involves choosing and creating a space where you will spend time reflecting on your life and your plant connections and meditating or journeying to connect with the essence or spirit of plants.

Within your sacred space you may also wish to create a special centrepiece, a kind of altar, where you can place certain objects like the plants you are working with or other objects that have special meaning for you.

Your space will evolve over time as you develop your connection with plant consciousness and will change depending on the seasons. For now, start with the basics and then you will find you naturally add elements and adjust your space to suit your style.

1. **Choose your spot.** If you are blessed with fine weather and a bug-free environment then by all means dedicate a specific space outside in your garden. I don't recommend choosing a place in a public area because you cannot guarantee that you will not be interrupted. Most people will have to set aside a small space in their living room, bedroom or study for their plant contemplation and meditation. This is totally fine; just make sure you cannot be interrupted and that there are no distractions. If you are lucky enough to already have an area of your living space that is dedicated to spiritual practice like yoga or meditation for example, this is perfect!

2. **Cleanse your space**. Before you use your space it is a good idea to clear away any unwanted energies that may have built up. Hold the intention to clear your space of negative energies and stagnant energy that is no longer needed.

Try some of the following and see what works for you:

- Light a candle (to bring in the light and banish darkness)
- Burn incense, or other traditional cleansing herbs like sage – see text below
- Play a drum loudly, clap your hands or play loud music
- Open windows
- Physically clean the space

- Use essential oils, in a spray or a diffuser; there's a huge variety so choose scents that you like with properties that appeal, frankincense encourages a meditative state and connects you to your higher self, lavender encourages relaxation and facilitates meditation, rose helps open the heart chakra and rosemary acts as a spiritual protector and promotes clarity.
- Cleanse the room with reiki or other healing energies
- Visualize divine light filling your space, taking away shadows and protecting you
- If you already work with spirit guides, angels or other beings of light or are open to the possibility of connecting with them, then invite them into your space to cleanse negative energies and protect you
- Say a space-clearing prayer

3. **Create your 'altar'.** This is not essential, just a suggestion for a way of dedicating a small space to the plants or other things that are important to you that you are trying to connect with. Think of it as a centrepiece, a focal point for your energy work.

   - Make your altar as ornate or as simple as you choose. You may like to use a windowsill, a small table, an area on your desk, a chair or even a tray that you can carry around and move from place to place. Since this altar will be themed around plants and nature, you can make it look lovely with flowers, leaves, plants, seeds, berries, aromatherapy oils or candles. This area will definitely change with the seasons and your personal preferences. Of course it goes without saying that a sacred altar or plant shrine outside is also a wonderful creation to build, and these areas will often be wilder and more natural, as they're exposed to the elements. Just experiment and do what you can – and more importantly, what you feel is necessary.
   - Add any object that makes you feel empowered and loved. The idea of an altar is to provide you with a focus point to encourage plant energies into your space. If you find you can do that by simply having a leaf or some other aspect of the plant with you on your bedside table, for example, then do that. You may like to use one particular house plant, or simply

feel drawn to certain images of plants; you can display these at home and at your workplace.

4. **Sit in your sacred space**. Test it out. How does it feel? Take out your journal and note down anything that you have observed, remembered or are feeling. Perhaps there is something missing; see what feels right.

5. **Remember you don't have to restrict the use of your sacred space to your work with plants**. Use your sacred space whenever you need to connect, relax, meditate or seek counsel. The more you spend time in your space, the more sacred and special it will feel.

Ideas for your altar and objects that you could add to your sacred space:

- Any object that makes you feel empowered and loved.
- Flowers, leaves, plants, seeds, berries, feathers to honour and invoke the spirit of the natural world.
- Aromatherapy oils or incense to invoke your sense of smell.
- Candles or fairy lights to honour the element of fire and create a magical ambience.
- Crystals and rocks to honour the element of earth and its strength.
- Spring water or holy water to honour the element of water and the emotions.
- Images, inspirational quotes or letters from loved ones.
- Display a chosen card for inspiration and guidance from your favourite deck; angel cards for example.

A sacred space is not dependent on the confines of physical space – shamanic practitioners and Druids create sacred space by calling in the sacred directions, which align with the directions of a compass and their corresponding elements in nature, colours, seasons of the year, stages of life, animals and plants.

Druids and other pagan belief systems may also cast a circle energetically by drawing the circle in the air or walking the circle and visualizing a circle of light. The focus and visualization involved in creating a circle in this way creates a powerful energetic container to hold the power and intention of whatever work is to take place within the space. A physical space, set aside for ritual, ceremony and contemplation, certainly helps anchor your focus, energies and attention when you are beginning your spiritual practice.

Honouring the Elements

The elements of nature can also be physically represented in your sacred space or on your altar to bring in their qualities. The following are some ideas and their corresponding directions. Note that this is different in different traditions; choose what feels right for you.

Air (in the east): May be represented by words that are spoken or written, prayers, songs; leaves or flowers; feathers or incense.

Fire (in the south): Often represented by a candle, a sunflower, movement, passion, fiery colours like red and orange or something creative such as a work of art.

Water (in the west): Water can be placed in a cup or represented by a lily, a shell, images of the moon, the ocean or a river.

Earth (in the north): Earth can be represented with a bowl of soil, crystals or stones. You can also use food such as bread, chocolate or nuts.

For my personal meditation and healing practice I like to use white sage or local herbs like mugwort and lavender to smudge and cleanse the area before I begin my work; the section below explains how to do this. I also like to light a candle and place the plant I am working with or a vase of flowers in season on my altar/focal point in the room. I always use reiki to cleanse and prepare my space and invite my guides and spirit helpers. In fact I invite a whole magical team of angels, ancestors and spirit guides to cleanse my space of negative and stagnant energies and help maintain an area that is safe, protected and full of light. I also like to imagine myself being encircled by a grove of trees; this feels protective and comforting.

Use whichever methods appeal and you are drawn to and, if you are working outside, you may like to ask a special tree to hold the space with you. Make sure you keep your space physically clean, tidy and fresh so that you are not encouraging energy to stagnate and hold you back.

Cleansing Space and Smudging

Dried herbs such as white sage, mugwort, wormwood or sweetgrass, sticks of palo santo and resins like copal and incense blends have been burned for centuries to shift negative or stagnant energy in order to cleanse, prepare and purify a ritual space, energy field or home and bring in the qualities of the plants being used. Burning plant material in this way is known as smudging and is a very powerful ritual.

Rather than simply burn the herbs or resins and waft the smoke around, the real potency will come when you connect to the invisible, to the spirit of the plant. Hold your intention in your mind to connect with the plant, asking that it brings its special quality to your space or your energy. All plants have different qualities that are said to, among many other things, cleanse, remove negative energy, help you stay grounded and encourage healing and connection with the spiritual realms. Select materials that you are drawn to, or that you can find locally, not just those that are sold generically. Pay close attention to how the materials burn – do they burn easily or do they seem reluctant? Sometimes sparks may fly or the fire may go out. Observe this behaviour; it carries a message for you and the way it burns indicates which qualities it embodies in your smudging ritual.

Ask the spirit of the plant to go to where it is needed; ask that truth be seen, heard, felt and spoken. Allow the spirit of the plant into your heart.

Feel into which plants you like to use and which ways may be appropriate for you to use them. Experiment with other plants that are growing locally to you. Make your own smudge sticks and incense.

SMUDGING PRAYER to Remove Stagnant Energies

May I be blessed and cleansed by the spirit of this plant.

May my heart be open to feel goodness and cleansed of bad feelings.

May my throat be free to speak my truth and cleansed of hurtful lies.

May my eyes be open to see the truth and cleansed of illusion.

May my ears be open to hear the truth and free from negative self-talk.

May my mind be awake to creative and kind thoughts and may it be cleansed of trickery.

May my hands be ready to create a beautiful life and cleansed of destruction.

May my feet be placed on my correct path and free from distraction.

May my body radiate with the divine light of the universe and shine.

May I be blessed and cleansed by the spirit of this plant.

Thank you, Thank you, Thank you.

A Grove of Trees

As you sit in your sacred space using whichever methods you feel drawn to in order to cleanse away any stagnant or dense energy, try the following method to feel support from nature. This practice was taught to me by Carol Day of the Centre for Creative Shamanism. Imagine a circle of trees surrounding you and your sacred space. The circle can be made up of different trees or the trees may be all the same shape and size. You may even like to surround that circle with another circle of trees for extra support and containment. At different times of the year you may wish to feel the energies of different trees. I often like to have particular trees at my back and at my front depending on the work that I am doing. Often I will experience one particular tree that stands out from the others; this always feels very supportive. As your experience with different plants broadens, you may find that you invite those plants in to spiritually surround your space.

Chapter Summary

The material covered in this chapter is an ongoing process as you flow with the natural rhythm of life's ups and downs. You will begin to know and become rooted in where you are and, most importantly, how you fit in with and are influenced by the natural world around you. It may seem disappointing that we haven't got down to the hands-on close encounters with plants yet, but be patient – this chapter together with the previous chapter both lay important foundations for authentic and grounded interaction so that appreciating the subtleties of plants will come with ease.

KEY POINTS

- Physically and emotionally attune yourself to where you live, the seasons and the cycles of the moon.
- Notice how the cycles of the natural world affect your world both outside and inside.
- Create physical sacred space to hold you as you explore and contemplate plant spirits.

In the next chapter we'll explore the sacred relationship that exists between plants and people and the role that you play. We will cover some of the many different ways in which plants can be incorporated into your life and also introduce the idea of a plant ally.

Plants and People:
Our Sacred Relationship

*"This world is indeed a living being endowed with a Soul
and intelligence… a single visible living entity containing all
other living entities, which by their nature are all related."*

— PLATO

Symbiotic relationships with plants are not only for pollinators; as humans, relying on oxygen to breathe, we are already in an important relationship with them. I know you've heard this before but it is a fact and worth thinking about: without plants to convert our carbon dioxide into oxygen, we would not have air to breathe.

It is also important to consider the microscopic plants that live on or near the ocean's surface and drift with the earth's current, known as phytoplankton, who are believed to contribute between 50 and 80 per cent of the earth's oxygen. We cannot survive without plants. There is an automatic bond between us.

When we breathe in oxygen, we breathe OUT carbon dioxide. Plants reverse the process; they need carbon dioxide to maintain all of their complex functions like growth and fluid transport and, as a by-product of these processes, they give off oxygen as a waste product. Which in turn we breathe.

This equation might remind you of your schooldays! The basic photosynthesis that occurs in plants looks like this:

carbon dioxide + water (+ light energy) → glucose + oxygen

What a perfect exchange nature has created.

So, without even being conscious of it, we are intensely linked by this fundamental natural process to the plant kingdom. When we start acknowledging plant consciousness, all we are doing is allowing ourselves to become more aware and conscious of the relationship that we already share with plants.

Let's also remember that we are not just bound to plants by our breath. All of our food comes either from plants directly or from animals that eat plant matter. Plants can create their tissue directly from sunlight but we depend on plants for the formation of ours. Each breath we take, our food, clothing and shelter are all down to plants.

Take a moment to reflect on all the opportunities that you have to interact with plants, through their products, both directly and indirectly over your day. Consider your breakfast cereal, morning cuppa, those tired office plants, the paper you print on and your cotton shirt.

Invisible Barriers

Despite being in an intense relationship with these conscious green beings that grow around us, most of us are complete strangers to them. We exist side by side with them, happily sharing the breath of life and yet most of us haven't even introduced ourselves and don't show the faintest bit of gratitude. What's more, we seem to have forgotten that unlike us, plants have been around on earth in some form or other for 400 billion years; and yet we act like we got here first! It feels like an invisible barrier has been erected over time that separates us from nature and distances us from our own essential nature. Our relationship has turned sour; we act like the earth is a resource at our service, rather than the co-creator of our destiny.

To begin to bridge this awkward unspoken divide, we can start by opening our hearts in acknowledgement, like a courtesy, holding the knowledge in our consciousness that we have a deep connection with plants that requires nurturing. It could be a simple case of introducing yourself the next time you pass a familiar plant. Saying 'Hi' as you would if you were trying to make a new acquaintance or expressing your admiration for how lovely a plant looks. In the next chapter, we will go into much more detail about different ways to do this when we go more deeply into exercises with plants.

A member of the Plant Spirit People group on Facebook shared how the atmosphere in her office completely shifted after she had taken the time to introduce herself to the plants there. A participant on one of my plant spirit workshops shared a similar story: following the workshop, she returned home with a new sense of connection to plants as conscious beings. As a result, she reconnected and introduced herself to the house plants in her flat and to her delight they responded. She said she now feels like she is sharing her home with two flatmates, not plants; they have conversations beyond the need to be watered and she has a real feel for the spirit of her plants.

Remember this one important idea: 'the guru is you.' Just as you have a unique vibration and a unique way of making and keeping human friends, you have your own way of having relationships and interaction with the plant world. So it's time to step up, claim your wisdom and ability to communicate with nature once again and restore your relationship with the plants around you.

Why Explore Your Relationship with Plants?

'It's been proven by quite a few studies that plants are good for our psychological development. If you green an area, the rate of crime goes down. Torture victims begin to recover when they spend time outside in a garden with flowers. So we need them, in some deep psychological sense, which I don't suppose anybody really understands yet.'

— JANE GOODALL

Feeling better is a key benefit of connecting to plants and spending time with nature. Studies are now showing us that green spaces help calm our nervous system, boost our immunity, improve our sleep and decrease blood pressure. Personally I find that as I expand my awareness and connect through my heart space with the consciousness of plants around me, I become conscious of something very much greater than myself. This realization that we are not alone, that we are part of a much larger and greater complex system of a living, breathing organism, is a great comfort.

I find also that in this heart space of expanded perspective, my compassion is extended towards all that we are connected to and resonate with. In other words, the more time we spend expanding our awareness to meet plant consciousness, the more compassion we feel towards the natural world; we will therefore have a greater respect for it and be less likely to bulldoze and pollute this wonderful resource! For me, it's like a dance: experimenting, observing, listening, feeling, creating patterns and flowing together so that I end up in a different place from where I first began. It's like creating a pathway that allows the beauty of the world to return into my heart.

Bridging the Gap – Ways to Incorporate Plants into Your Life

No wonder we feel so good in nature! Plants are not only beautiful and often highly fragrant; they are also an incredibly versatile and accessible element of a holistic approach to health and well-being. Living allies, they provide medicine that is powerful and full of vitality; we can work with plants physically, emotionally and spiritually. All of these ways help us to directly experience the plant, form a relationship, start dancing together and feel our way towards health and wholeness. You may already use plants in these ways, but if some are new to you, test them out:

- Cleansing and creating sacred space as discussed in Chapter 3.
- Herbal medicine: using the physical properties of medicinal plants to heal physical symptoms and ailments, in forms like tinctures, salves, infusions and capsules.
- Plant essences: using the vital force of the plant for healing emotional and spiritual malaise, in forms such as the Bach flower essences.
- Homeopathy: a complementary health care system, based on the principle of like cures like, in which the majority of remedies are plant-based.
- Essential oils: extracted oils containing the aromatic qualities of a plant, with many uses ranging from treating physical and emotional health issues to room or product fragrance.
- Nourishing herbal infusions and teas: part of daily health and self-care. Popular kinds include peppermint and nettle – not to mention your morning brew! (although herbal teas and infusions can be a delicious alternative if you're trying to cut down on caffeine).
- Meditation in nature to feel grounded, connected and supported.
- Ceremony, ritual and prayer – asking for the support of plant spirits or blessing.
- Plant spirit healing: working with the spirit of the plants to restore balance, well-being and vitality so that we can be more fully who we are and live according to our own true nature.
- Growing (and eating) vegetables, fruits and herbs as part of a healthy and sustainable lifestyle.

- Creating beautiful outdoor spaces with plants for sanctuary, structure and beauty (and indoor ones too!.
- Purifying the air in office environments with indoor plants like peace lilies and ferns.
- Lifting our spirits and bringing joy – think of giving flowers to those who are unwell.
- Nature's design; being inspired by the intricate pattern, colour, shape and style of the plant kingdom to influence the design of, for example, our interiors and clothing.
- Natural materials for textiles like cotton, silk and hemp and everyday products like cardboard and paper.

Meeting Plants and Exploring Plant Personalities

Each plant has its own personality, just like us! I like to encourage students to seek relationships with plants and know plants and their medicines for themselves, rather than simply reading everything from books. This is because plants can seem to behave in different ways, perhaps highlighting different aspects of themselves to different people.

This may seem slightly confusing but let's look at it this way.

My name is Fay Johnstone. I behave and am perceived differently when I am with different people but I am still fundamentally the same Fay Johnstone as I always will be. For example, to my parents I am a beautiful, successful and loving daughter who has caused them many sleepless nights. To my old college friends I am a slightly bonkers and down-to-earth pal who laughs ridiculously and dresses flamboyantly and always has an unbelievable story to tell. To my former colleagues in the corporate world I was a hard-working professional who was a bit of a stress case on the verge of a meltdown. To my students and clients I am an avid plant person, a sensitive healer and practical medicine woman.

Different aspects of me are noticed by different people and I choose to show different aspects of my personality and gifts with different people. Sometimes I might choose this by what I judge as appropriate; sometimes it might simply be a case of trust and what I feel comfortable revealing to others about myself. In my experience plants behave exactly like this too.

A few years ago, during early spring in Nova Scotia, I introduced some friends to motherwort for the first time – with surprising results.

It was early spring and still no green was to be seen across the land. However, in my small greenhouse I had kept a few of my favourite herbs indoors over the winter. One evening I took a small potted motherwort plant to my women's circle. Her presence simply fascinated the women and many recognized her matronly energy and wished to honour her. One lady took her rattle and spent a while rattling around motherwort, who was visibly excited, pleased with the attention and enjoying the gentle rattle. It was fascinating to see the two make their connection.

Another woman decided to journey to the spirit of motherwort and when she did so she simply wept, finding the connection so strong, so deep and so authentic that it overwhelmed her.

These two encounters demonstrate how the same plant can create, even at the same time, highly diverse reactions in people as each person experiences a plant through their own personal filter. And on an individual level, your perception of the plant will be slightly different each time, even if you have met it hundreds of times before.

Whenever I am encouraging herbal students to research the actions and uses of a particular herb, like most other herbalists I recommend as a good rule of thumb looking up the same herb in at least three different sources. The main characteristics and actions of the herb in question will be covered by all these sources and you will most likely also find that there are different suggestions put forward by different authors depending on the preferences of the author and their experience with that particular remedy.

Experiment for yourself. As you start to become more familiar with plants you may absorb reams of information, like downloads, relating to the plants, which is personal to you and relates to your experience of the plant or a current challenge you are facing. After all, it is this personal experience of a plant that is relevant to you, not second-hand information. Always keep the door of your perception open and child-like, free of judgement. Often we can limit our experience of a plant by what we think we know about it. Instead keep the possibility alive that the plant might be exactly the answer you are looking for. For example, if dandelion is trying to grab your attention then let it; don't dismiss it because you think you know what its healing qualities are. Don't miss the subtle nuances of its personality by letting judgement limit your experiences.

EXERCISE Plant Speed Dating

The key word for this exercise is 'speed'; you are going to spend three minutes outside with five different plants in quick succession, visiting them in their natural habitat. Spend a moment outside seeking out plants that might be willing volunteers for this exercise. Breathe into your heart space before you begin.

- Visit the first plant where it is growing and make a note of your first impression of it. This might be one word, for example 'beautiful', or something more complex.
- Take a coloured pen or pencil and quickly sketch a pattern or squiggle to represent how that plant makes you feel.
  Does it feel positive or negative? Interesting or dull?
- Then when the time is up, thank the plant and move to the next one.
- After you have spent three minutes with five plants, compare your first impressions and sketches of them all.
- Consider which plants you would like to take on a second date.

Plant Allies

To understand what makes a plant ally, think of a friend whose vibration resonates with you. Then also think along the lines of spirit helper, angel guide, ancestral spirit, power animal or spirit guide. A being that is your partner for healing, growth and transformation, like a spirit guide, who you can rely on for support for certain issues or challenges, like a great friend.

The wonderful thing about plants is that they are living allies; so, as well as connecting to their spirit or their vibration for wisdom, guidance, teaching and healing, you can also benefit from their physical presence – you can grow and cultivate the plant, physically touch it, observe, smell, taste, admire and really explore the plant with all of your senses. The benefits of this include being able to create magical medicines for healing and well-being, thanks to their physical properties, and countless more inspired botanical creations. I often carry a plant in my pocket, for example, or make a plant essence.

Plant allies can be a personal guide and friend for a short time or a lifetime depending on what you are needing in the moment. And remember, plants are not humans and don't follow our rules or ways, so interacting with them will not always be predictable or provide us with the outcomes that we were expecting. But that is half the fun of the adventure.

I am often asked who is my plant ally and it is always a very hard question to answer because I don't want to miss anyone out. I found that as soon as I had the intention in my heart to get to know plants in a more holistic and meaningful way, there were many green friends trying to grab my attention and offering assistance. While living in Nova Scotia, during the summer months we were surrounded by fields of red clover and yarrow. These two plants taught me a lot about healing, grounding, finding the power of my heart and protection from the drama of others. My relationship with red clover is less powerful now because it doesn't grow readily in my local area. On the other hand, yarrow is everywhere and has really stepped forward as a powerful, strong ally for me and for that I am truly grateful. I often wear a small potion bottle containing yarrow elixir round my neck to help me feel the presence of this protective ally.

Questions for Self-reflection

1. Imagine a world in which humans and the plant kingdom have equal respect for each other and work together. How would life be different?
2. What do you envision co-creating with plants? Would this be a beautiful garden, a healthy vegetable patch, a thriving community woodland? Medicinal potions, healing essences, or magical herbs for the kitchen?
3. Imagine you could speak freely to plants and understand clearly what messages they were communicating to you. What questions would you ask? How would your life be different? What do you think the plants might say to you? How might they communicate this to you and what would you do with this information?
4. How do you think plants could help you or help the world in general?
5. Is there a specific plant that you already consider an ally or one that you would like to explore further?

Chapter Summary

The idea of this chapter was to draw your attention to the sacred relationship that you are already enjoying with the plant kingdom.

KEY POINTS

- Become conscious of the sacred relationship between humans and plants.
- Think about the different ways that you can incorporate plants into your life.
- Consider plants as people, with different personalities and follies.
- Be willing to open your heart to a new plant friend, an ally to support and guide you.

The following chapter examines your mindset and helps you identify those attitudes and behaviours which may be hindering your connection with the plant kingdom.

Co-creating with Nature:
Adopting the Right Mindset

*"I am a thousand winds that blow. I am the diamond glints
on snow. I am the sunlight on ripened grain. I am the gentle
autumn rain. When you awaken in the morning's hush,
I am the swift uplifting rush of quiet birds in circled flight.
I am the soft stars that shine at night...."*

— **MARY ELIZABETH FRYE**, from
"Do Not Stand at My Grave and Weep"

Indigenous people from many cultures across the globe have long recognized the interconnectedness of people with the natural world; but somewhere along the line, in the more industrialized West, we got it into our heads that nature is outside of us and we pushed it away. We've adopted an 'us and them' approach to the natural world. We have lost the intimacy that we once enjoyed when our lifestyles tied us more closely to the land. Our protective walls, that keep us inside, conveniently act as a barrier between us and the creative, often unpredictable dance of nature outside. However, the more time you spend in your heart space and consider how separate our relationship with nature has become the more ridiculous and uncomfortable you will feel about the situation.

Plants dominate our landscape, the biomass of plants on land has been estimated to be around 1,000 times that of animals. We are born of this earth, we survive on the air and food of this earth and when we die our bodies will become of the earth. So this detachment that we have created, this separation, is false and damaging. It's time to change our mindset and step out of the ego mind that thinks it has dominion over the natural world into a mindset that views plants as equal partners. In this way we open ourselves up to exploring a landscape that is full of conscious beings filled with intelligence (that may be greater than our own) and the wisdom of the ages. A level playing field like this opens up possibilities for us to learn great things from plants and also dive deeper into the web that interconnects us all.

While my partner and I were running the farm this was a real challenge, especially when faced with limited time and resources. There were many times when I caught myself wanting the plants to behave in a certain way, or flower on demand to suit a wedding that was coming up.

I also think fondly of a friend, Sarah, who was telling me a story about how she had tried three times to plant a clematis in a certain corner of the garden. Despite the growing conditions being right and the plants appearing healthy at first, each time the clematis had died. She had persisted, replacing the plant another two times; it never occurred to her that the plant might not want to grow there and there might be a reason beyond obvious growing conditions for why the plant wasn't surviving.

Fortunately we have begun to change our view of plants. Plant neurobiology demonstrates that plants are dynamic and highly sensitive organisms that actively and competitively forage for resources, accurately compute their circumstances and make decisions; they recognize self and non-self, have memory and demonstrate territorial behaviour. We have more in common with plants than we think.

I believe that in order to befriend our green allies once again, we need to offer our hearts in equal partnership rather than maintain an attitude of 'I am greater than you are'. Being grateful and appreciative is a much more attractive state of being. In my experience we only have to regard plants with reverence and gratitude to unlock their wisdom and strength.

EXERCISE Acknowledging Nature

Take a walk outside in nature; allow yourself five minutes to physically land in the green space and mentally arrive. Breathe deeply into your whole body, focusing especially on your heart. With each exhale and each step further into nature, allow yourself to relax a little bit more.

When you feel ready, start opening up your whole sense of awareness to the green that grows outside and surrounds you as you walk. Notice trees, plants, flowers, weeds and grass; whatever you can see that is green and growing.

Recognize now that all of this green that surrounds you is conscious, just like you. Recognize now that all that grows around you is communicating in some way. Let these thoughts sink into your mind and also into your heart and your wider awareness. How does that make you feel? Where do you feel this in your body? Find a way that resonates for you to open up and say 'Hello' in acknowledgement of all the green beings that are surrounding you. You may want to say the words out loud, or in a whisper. You may wish to pause by a tree or another plant of interest and reach your hand out in acknowledgement. Spend as long as you need out in nature like this. When you are ready to leave, offer your thanks.

How Do We Approach Plants and Gauge Right Relationship?

Right relationship, or in other words 'appropriate behaviour', is key to all relationships really but most especially to those with our friends in the plant kingdom. Imagine meeting someone for the first time from an unfamiliar culture, who spoke a new language that you hadn't mastered, but you were just hoping to wing it.

You might feel nervous, hesitant, confused or even frightened at times; and the same goes for when you are approaching how to meet a plant. My advice is to go steady, be respectful, open and non-judgemental, act thoughtfully and, if you don't understand something or receive a response, then ask again in a different way. There is no need to get frustrated or rush into things; learning a new language isn't easy and does not come instantly.

Sometimes you might come across a beautiful plant that intrigues you and that you desperately wish to befriend, but when you approach you get the distinct feeling that you are not welcome. No problem! There could be many reasons that the plant isn't in the mood to interact with you, so just leave it alone for another day.

Guidelines When Meeting a Plant

Whenever you are working with plants, planting, weeding, harvesting or just admiring as you take a walk in nature, I suggest getting into the habit of treating a plant as you would a person. Meeting plants is a lot like meeting people and, while I am not going to give you a manual on how to make friends, the following may act as helpful pointers. Most importantly, feel into your heart space for what is appropriate.

1. **Introduce yourself (out loud)** i.e. 'Hello, my name is Fay.'
2. **Show appreciation to the plant** i.e., 'It's great to meet you, thank you for having me in your home today. You look radiant.'

3. **Present an offering.** See following text for suggested offerings.
4. **State your intention.** 'I would like to get to know you better', or 'I would like to harvest some of your leaves to make an infused oil at home to help heal my skin.' Or if gardening, 'I am going to trim some of your branches to give the other plants more light.'
5. **Spend as much time with the plant as you need, doing what you need to do – breathing, observing, listening deeply. Feel into the space between you.** Note down everything: observations/sensations in your body, colours, feelings, memories, thoughts that come and go.
6. **Really let the plant into your heart, visualize it there and love it.** Note down how you think the plant is feeling and how you feel about the plant.
7. **Always ask permission to touch, taste and smell the plant** – if it doesn't feel right then don't do it! Use your common sense where taste is concerned. Place a small amount on your tongue and chew – if it feels prickly or odd then SPIT IT OUT!
8. **You may feel the urge to place the plant on an area of your body to receive its energy** – see what you experience.
9. **Always give thanks** and leave the area as untouched as it was when you first arrived.
10. **Consider ways that you could interact with the plant further.** What does it inspire in you? What can you do for the plant?

Respect and Exchange:
Appropriate Offerings

When initiating any contact with nature I have always found it extremely beneficial to leave an offering as I begin my work. Sometimes I will even feel compelled to leave offerings while out on a walk, simply to honour the beauty that surrounds me and show my appreciation. It is a wonderful habit to get into.

Leaving offerings as you begin working with plants and carrying out the exercises in this book is a signal to the natural world of your respect and intent. You can also view it as a pre-payment, since you are hoping to communicate with them and are offering your thanks in advance for their willingness and expressing your gratitude.

What Can You Offer?

Sometimes a plant simply appreciates love, attention and a little water, but you can also consider the question 'What would satisfy the plant?'

Some of my regular offerings include:

- holy water
- flower petals
- milk
- honey
- sugar
- seeds or corn
- olive oil
- wine, beer or water
- herbs
- fresh flowers
- chocolate
- pennies
- tobacco (Grow your own tobacco plants from heritage seed or find someone who does rather than support the tobacco industry.)

Always be mindful when leaving offerings. Don't leave out plastic cups, non-biodegradable items or, in an urban or busy area, food like chocolate that may be harmful to people and their pets. If you are going to tie a ribbon to the branch of a tree, do it loosely, so the plant has room to grow.

Offering Your Actions

You don't always have to give objects; your intent and actions can be as powerful as a physical offering. For example, every place will appreciate someone who picks up litter or works to protect an area of natural beauty. The gift of responsible action can be a great gift for a place as a whole and it goes without saying that living responsibly, caring for the planet that we live on, does the same.

So, as you turn your lights off and heating thermostat down, dedicate your action to Mother Earth. Plants respond really well to sound, so often I find myself singing and dancing in their presence too, or offering a poem. Don't give begrudgingly; give because you want to, give from the heart. Think about what is appropriate for you to offer.

MEDITATION Growing from Seed

The idea of this meditation is to shift your perspective and experience life from a plant's point of view. It is a great meditation for grounding oneself and connecting to Mother Earth, so feel free to use it whenever necessary. Do it from a comfortable position in your sacred space or a place where you will not be disturbed. Afterwards note down any experiences, sensations and observations.

Settle yourself comfortably, either sitting on a chair or cushion or lying down. Take a few moments to gather yourself in and really become present where you are. Leave the business and demands of your day outside this sacred space, close your eyes and focus your attention inwards. Notice the natural rhythm of your breath as it flows in and out. With each breath allow yourself to relax a little more.

If you are seated, roll back your shoulders and pay attention to your posture so you sit with dignity, allowing your head to float upwards to the heavens.

With each breath allow your shoulders to relax a bit more and let this relaxation flow throughout your body.

As you breathe in imagine light flowing in with your breath and spreading throughout your entire body.

Breathe out any worries or pain being held in your body.

If your mind wanders, it's no problem; just refocus on your breath. Gently breathing in and gently breathing out, enjoy the peaceful flow of your breath in each moment.

As you breathe in, focus on your heart centre and allow the breath to open up your heart a little more. Breathe out any tension or resistance that you find there.

Breathe in and focus on your heart centre once more, imagining white light flowing into your heart and illuminating it, allowing it to open a little more.

Breathe out any tension or discomfort that may be present. Continue focusing on your heart as you breathe. When you feel ready, begin the meditation as follows.

Imagine yourself as a tiny plant seed, nestled into the damp ground. You are tiny yet full of potential. Consider this for a moment. Get yourself nice and cosy in the earth; enjoy the feeling of being surrounded by Mother Earth with everything that you need.

Experience the knowing that you are capable of growing big and strong from your tiny seed.

Experience the knowing of who you are, where you come from and what you will become.

It's time to use your energy to sprout.

Sense the light around you, enticing you out of your dark cave. Does it feel exciting? Scary? How does it feel to be tempted to be drawn out of the cosy darkness?

Take the leap and sprout out into the light. Burst into the open air. Sense the freshness and brightness that surrounds you.

Feel the sense of space that surrounds you.

Bathe in the light and bask in the sense of freedom and new possibilities that this brings.

Now feel into the roots that grow beneath you.

You are growing roots that spread deep down into the earth, searching for nourishment. These roots make you strong and provide foundation for your growth.

These strong roots communicate and network around you.

Enjoy sensing in to your root system as it holds you to the earth.

As you breathe allow yourself to grow larger, more solid and more branching. How are you growing? Perhaps you are becoming furry, smooth, firm, hard, shiny, soft, floaty.

How does it feel to change in this way? Remember when you were so small? What do your leaves look like? Are you in bud?

Now sense into the cycle of the day. We will begin in spring.

Imagine heavy dew all around you and sunrise lifts the darkness and the day begins, the heat of the sun and the business of the day unfurls.

What can you see going on around you? Are animals and insects visiting your leaves or flowers? What does this feel like? Are you relaxed or threatened?

Is life noisy or quiet? What does the sun feel like on your surface?

What about the rain? Does it feel refreshing, is your thirst quenched?

Now as the sun goes down in the west the day is ending and the ground and air become cooler. Are you still busy transporting food and nutrients or are you resting?

Let's time-travel into summertime; how is this different to spring? What are your energies focusing on now? Are you in flower and inviting bees to pollinate you? Do you have enough to drink and nourish you?

Is the earth around you dry? Are your roots busy stretching to find water and nutrients?

As the year moves into autumn, what is going on from your perspective? Do you have fruits to harvest? Does anyone or anything pay attention to you?

Do you communicate with other plants? What does it feel like being rooted to the same spot for your whole life, connected strongly to Mother Earth but only seeing something from that particular spot?

The cold darkness of winter is upon you now.

Are you an annual plant that just lives for one year? If so, how has your life been?

Or are you perennial, around for as long as you can manage, preparing to brace yourself for the cold winter ahead, sending your energy down into the roots of the earth?

What will the winter be like for you? Will a cool blanket of snow envelop you, will there be harsh frosts and freezing winds to whip your leaves and break them away? How can it be that you remain standing in these conditions?

And how do you know to send out green shoots again in the spring?

Breathe into the clarity and inner wisdom contained in this plant that was once a tiny seed. Breathe into the strength, energy and resilience that these green allies possess.

Sense their beauty, smell their freshness, experience their earthiness and strength in their connection to Mother Earth.

Keep your roots in Mother Earth, stay grounded...

Return your focus to your breath, enjoying the flow as you breathe in and out gently.

When you feel ready to return to the world, start to wriggle your hands, wrists and ankles, then your knees and elbows, to wake up your body gently. Stretch your arms above your head, stretch out your whole body.

Place your hands over your eyes and open your eyes behind your palms. Take your hands away when you are ready to see the world again.

Return to your day with the wisdom of the seed in your heart. Think of yourself as a special seed. How do you need to be nourished so you can blossom and grow so that the world can reap your gifts?

Access the meditation at **www.plantsthatspeak.com.**

Questions for Self-reflection

1. Consider your daily actions towards plants and the natural world; are your actions in harmony with your perceived attitude towards the environment?
2. Do your actions reflect an attitude of co-creation? Where are you still operating from the viewpoint of 'dominion over' or 'I am greater than you are'?
3. Do you recycle? Do you make buying choices based on the environmental impact of the corporation that your purchases support?
4. How can you reduce your use of plastic? How can you make more sustainable choices for the environment?
5. How do you act towards plants? Are you respectful, nonchalant, do you even notice plants around you?
6. Do you get annoyed with the weeds in your garden? If so, what can you do differently?
7. Do you want certain plants in your garden to perform in a certain way?

Chapter Summary

This chapter was all about helping you examine your mindset towards plants, understand how to meet a plant and expand your heart to a place of co-creation and partnership with the plant kingdom.

KEY POINTS

- Be aware of appropriate behaviour and right relationship.
- Reflect on what you can offer in gratitude to the plants you meet.
- Adjust your mindset and actions; are they aligned with your desire to connect authentically with the plants around you?

You have been patient enough; now, from your heart space and with an open attitude of co-creative partnership, let's go forward and connect with plants using all your physical senses. This really is the best part – I hope you enjoy it!

PART TWO

BUILDING PLANT
RELATIONSHIPS

∽

PRACTICAL STEPS
TO OPEN YOUR SENSES
TO THE
NATURAL WORLD

Sensory Exploration

"Each stone, each bend cries welcome to him.
He identifies with the mountains and the streams,
he sees something of his own soul in the plants
and the animals and the birds of the field."

— **PAULO COELHO**, from *The Warrior of the Light*

Building a conscious relationship with plants helps you to remember the truth of who you are and feel a sense of connection that provides new insight and a fresh way to look at the world. Once we are touched by the natural world it starts to have more meaning and purpose; we can better appreciate its value and hold it dear to us.

Since we are nature and so are plants, we do have the capacity for learning the language of nature and communicating – it is just a case of taking the time to remember and retrain ourselves. You can't learn this type of relationship from reading books or watching videos. You need first-hand personal interaction with plants to get out of your usual mindset and decipher the more rhythmic patterns and subtle ways of communication with nature. This requires an intimate knowing and experience of nature that is unique to you.

In order to do this effectively, you need to throw your judgements, preconceived ideas and knowledge of plants out of the window. Start with an open heart, a childlike curious mind and a willingness to meet a companion on a level playing field. Get ready to expand your consciousness and interact with the plants on all levels, starting with a full-body immersion using all your physical senses. It's a case of feeling your way with the touch of your heart rather than the touch of your fingers.

Come to Your Senses

The language of plants comes in many forms, many more than we can really conceive when we are stuck in our usual mindset, so start by dropping your awareness down from your head into your heart and open up your senses and doors of perception, as if you were aligning your heartbeat with the heartbeat of nature. Remember to feel first (from your heart) and think later. Let's consider each plant as an expression of consciousness that is communicating with us. How might they be doing this? Colour, appearance, shape, size, location, movement, growth pattern, form, texture, taste, sound and fragrance are all obvious methods of communication that we can easily pick up on and explore, once we start opening up our senses and grounding into our body.

Perhaps you have a sense or some that are better developed than the others? Where do you receive your most trusted information – is it through your eyes or ears? Are you drawn to texture or sensitive to sound? Do you find that in certain situations you might have a feeling, like a gut feeling or an inner knowing? Generally I would call myself a very visual person; however, when I am tuning in to plants, it is another sense completely that takes over. I often physically sense the presence of a plant, like a crackle in the atmosphere at a certain frequency. I also find that I get very emotional when a plant has a clear and important message to communicate to me.

When we are interacting with plants (or anyone for that matter), being fully present is key. It's especially important for plant communication because the nuances of nature are so subtle that if we are not paying attention then we will miss the message. Likewise, when we are too caught up in our ego and personal agenda, we can easily misinterpret messages and communication.

Fortunately, as discussed in Chapter 2, self-awareness is a skill that we can develop through meditation and mindfulness practices. If you haven't already begun a meditation practice, start with a minimum of five minutes a day to get you in the habit of being still and being able to observe the thoughts that occur in your mind rather than let them run away with you. Many practices use the breath as an anchor as the focus of your attention.

EXERCISE **Body Scan**

The body scan is a practice that involves mindfully sweeping your awareness over your entire body to help you become fully present in your body and bring awareness to what is present within it. This exercise is great training for being fully present to and aware of the sensations that arise in your body, which are key abilities for plant communication.

Ensure that you will be undisturbed for about half an hour. Lie down on a bed or on the floor, but be careful that you're not too comfortable or you may fall asleep! If necessary, cover yourself with a blanket to keep warm.

Close your eyes to turn your attention inwards and focus for a while on the rising and falling of the breath in your body. Simply breathe deeply right into the centre of your being and exhale as far out as you can before beginning again.

Take long, calming breaths, allowing yourself to relax a little more with each exhalation, releasing what is no longer needed. Envisage each inhalation renewing your body with fresh breath and new opportunity. Ride the rhythm of the breath as it flows throughout your body like waves on the ocean. Sense into your body as a whole from head to toe, noticing where your body begins and ends, feeling yourself weighed down by gravity onto the floor.

Begin by bringing your attention to your big toes and explore the sensations that you find here. Gradually extend your awareness to include your other toes and the whole of your feet. Allow your feet to relax, send your breath down into your feet and imagine your breath as a warm, comforting beam of light.

Little by little expand the light and send your breath into your ankles and then up your legs, focusing on your calves, knees and thighs. Each time, allow your muscles to soften and relax. Bring your attention to both legs, allowing all the muscles to release tension. Take your awareness upwards, sweeping over your hips and pelvic area. Breathe in loving light and allow the organs and muscles in these areas to relax. Let yourself release any tension or energy that you are holding here. Keep expanding your awareness up your body to include your digestive system. Breathe here, allowing light to shine in and release any tension that you are holding. Continue upwards slowly, releasing tension in your lungs, your chest, the whole of your abdomen and the whole of your upper body. If one area seems more resistant than the others, then stay here longer breathing into the area and allowing tension to leave with each exhalation.

Pay close attention to your shoulders and neck, softly breathing light and love into this area and giving yourself permission and sufficient time to relax.

Follow your awareness down into your arms, elbows, wrists, hands and to your fingertips. Sense into the warmth and energy that is stored in the palms of your hands. Feel the relief that they are at rest. Breathe light and love from your shoulders down into both arms and release any tension that remains.

From your neck, notice where your spine meets your head and slowly draw your attention to your head, neck, throat and face. Release tension held in the muscles around the forehead, the eyes and jaw. Notice any other sensations in your face and allow it to soften with the light of your breath and your awareness. Expand your awareness to encompass the whole of your head, including the scalp and crown. Breathe into your entire head and imagine it full of light. From here scan quickly over your body again, from the tips of your toes up to the crown of the head, sending your breath and light to every cell. Feel the flow of the breath as it rises and falls in your body. Notice how you feel physically and emotionally, but leave your judgement aside. Envisage all the cells in your body breathing together.

When you feel ready to finish, start by slowly moving your toes and fingers, ankles and wrists. Stretch your arms above your head and stretch out your whole body. Place your hands over your eyes and open your eyes behind your palms before taking the hands away. Gently bring yourself up to a sitting position and take a few breaths here. Pay attention to your feelings and give yourself a few moments before you dash back into your day. If you can, try to maintain this awareness of your body as you go about your daily routine.

You can also listen to this at: **www.plantsthatspeak.com.**

Using the Body's 'Radar'

When we are fully in our body and aware of how it feels, we can more easily pick up the subtle communications that may come from our surroundings like the plants, people or spaces that we are hanging out with. For example, if you are suddenly aware of a warmth, a tingling or a slight pull, or perhaps even pain, in an area of your body, this is worth noting as your body may be tuning in to something that the plant is communicating to you. It can also be helpful to tune in to how our body feels to distinguish physical sensations from emotional feelings or concerns that we are carrying. It takes practice to finely tune your body in to this 'radar' because if you suffer from mental chatter it can be a real challenge to calm and refocus your mind. We spend so much time in our heads that for many people, being grounded in the body, awake to its sensations, is a new experience. You will need to figure out what being present in your body feels like for you before you can use this radar to feel into the subtle communications from plants. Mindful movement practices like yoga, Five Rhythms, walking meditation and movement medicine will help you cultivate this familiarity with being in your body.

Your Place of Knowing

Another way of looking at this idea, is finding your place of knowing. I'm referring to that still place inside of you, that voice, feeling, sensation or sound that simply *knows*. It's a feeling of solidity and trust that comes from our soul. I access this space through meditation, breath work and grounding into the earth.

Think about times in your life when you have simply known, been sure about something or had a gut feeling. How can you recognize this feeling in your body and what can you do more of to cultivate your connection with this place of knowing?

EXERCISE Self-awareness Check-in

> Before you start to work with plants or carry out any of the exercises that follow, to help you tune in to your awareness take out your journal and note down your thoughts and feelings; ask yourself – how am I feeling today?
>
> To simplify this, especially if you are short on time, you may want to answer with one-word responses, thinking in terms of how you are feeling physically, intellectually, emotionally and spiritually. Doing this helps us check in with not only what is going on for us physically but also what lies beneath the surface. I have Women Within International to thank for introducing me to this exercise.
>
> For example:
> How am I feeling right now? And where do I feel this in my body?
> How am I physically feeling? For example, I'm tired and sore in my shoulders.
> What is on my mind? For example, I'm confused and overloaded, have lots going on in my head.
> What is my core emotion? For example, I'm anxious and I feel this in my throat area.

How am I feeling spiritually? For example, I feel connected; I sense this in my feet.

If negative responses are coming up for you, refrain from judgement. Resist the temptation to block, suppress or hide negative responses, thoughts and feelings; instead, just allow your responses to surface and note them down. Also, refrain from analyzing your feelings; this is purely an observation exercise. Listen to your body and be sure to note any dreams, songs or memories that are on your mind too.

EXERCISE Self-awareness Review

After completing any plant connection, take time to tune in to yourself and once again revisit the self-reflection questions above and compare your responses with those from before your plant connection. Ask yourself: what is shifting? What is flowing? What am I moving towards or away from? Am I experiencing any resistance?

Also note any thoughts or feelings that you remember from the plant encounter and any other observations that have come up since.

Keep your journal close to your bedside so you can note down any dreams that may follow. Also make a note of any omens and signs; these might be in the form of flavours, scents or even plants, or environmental and health issues that come up in conversation, in the media or in other areas of your life.

Developing Peripheral Awareness

In today's world, there is so much directly in front of our faces that demands our urgent attention that we don't often make much use of our peripheral awareness. This basically means your awareness of what surrounds you in space, i.e., everything that you are not actually looking straight at.

To successfully work with plants out in nature, it is worth developing this peripheral awareness. Science is now finding that our peripheral awareness links to a unique circuit in the brain that affects how we move and how we feel. When our peripheral vision shrinks (as in tunnel vision), we feel threatened and our stress levels rise.

We spend so much time focused on the tiny screens in front of us that our peripheral vision has become rather ignored and underused. When working with plants, even though we sometimes might have in mind a particular plant that we are 'on the hunt' for, it's always beneficial to activate and pay attention to your peripheral vision. Often, the plant we are most in need of for personal healing, or that we require as the missing ingredient for our herbal preparation or essence, is the plant that we will notice out of the corner of our eye. At this edge of our vision is where the magic happens, so put down this book for a moment, stare at an object straight in front of you and practise seeing out of the corners of both eyes. What can you see without moving?

Start developing your peripheral vision now, so you can maintain a holistic viewpoint on your world, a greater perspective on the dramas that play out before you and an eye for the magic that happens at the corner of your vision and is desperate to get your attention.

EXERCISE Sitting Practice Using Peripheral Senses

Take a seat outside on a park bench or at a cafe. Look straight ahead of you and don't move your eyes. Make a mental note of everything that you can see without moving your eyes or head. Include that which you see before you and in your peripheral vision.

After a few minutes note down everything that you have seen.

Repeat the exercise and see if you can add to your list.

EXERCISE Walking Practice Using Peripheral Senses

Take a walk that you know well – a short walk of around 10–20 minutes will do. Make sure it's a walk that you have done many times so you don't need to be fully focused on where you are heading, but instead your body wants to go there automatically and at least partly knows its way.

Begin to walk slowly and as you walk bring your awareness to the periphery of your vision; with no expectations just notice, out of the corners of your eyes, what moves, notice what plants and objects seem to be trying to grab your attention.

Enjoy your walk and note down afterwards what you have noticed.

Repeat the same walk later that day or week, doing the same exercise, and notice if the same plants are calling your attention, or if there is something new that you hadn't noticed before.

Is there anything worth investigating?

Beginning the Dance:
Allowing a Plant to Choose You

For each of these exercises and those that follow throughout the book that require you to work with plants, I recommend allowing a plant to choose you. To enable this process, get yourself outside among the plants that you wish to work with and hold in your heart the intention for choosing one. You may find it useful to write down the intention to help clarify it in your heart.

Prepare by using the self-awareness check-in exercise above if that is working for you. If you don't find that works, be sure instead to spend at least five minutes in meditation and note down your thoughts and feelings and any other observations in your journal that come to mind before you begin your hunt for a plant.

Take a slow walk through the area that you are going to be working in and just notice, using your peripheral vision, which plant is trying to get your attention. You may find, if you have set aside some time to do these exercises, that the intention for finding a plant to work with has already been at work as you go about your day, so you may have already had little signs and nudges from plants that are jumping forward to work with you. Be relaxed and in the moment as you walk, go slowly and keep your eyes and heart open. To keep you focused and prevent your mind from wandering off, focus on your breath as an anchor. Try to remain open to who will step forward to work with you and prepare for anyone – large or small.

When you feel you have been 'chosen' by a plant, honour that choosing, whether it is what you expected or not, and approach the plant. Feel into the connection and breathe. If it feels like a good fit then stay with the plant. Sometimes it might feel odd or awkward; this could indicate an area with which you need great healing and are experiencing a little resistance. No problem – if you don't feel like going there, play with something easier and revisit that plant when you are feeling ready.

How Do You Touch Me?

My favourite exercise to do when approaching a plant for the first time is to ask the question 'How do you touch me?' I experienced this exercise at the Pishwanton Centre in the Scottish Borders, with a wild rose bush, and I always include it on my workshops because our first impressions are so striking.

You'll need a small, about A5-sized, piece of paper and coloured pencils or similar (I like to use pastels because they are rough and easily smudged and blended). Ask yourself the above question and then create a pattern of colour on the page. You may come up with a squirl, wavy lines, dots, splodges, or you may even write down words that leap up at you from your first impressions of the plant. The idea is not to draw a physical representation of the plant in front of you, but to capture something that touches you, which is why colour can be so useful.

I remember a workshop that I held one very sunny March day just south of Edinburgh at the Secret Herb Garden. We were doing this exercise as a group by a beautiful willow tree that was bursting to life with fluffy catkins and swarming with bees that had just woken up after a long winter. The effect was awe-inspiring – it was noisy, busy, literally humming with life and vitality, a joyful representation of spring energy. The whole group were inspired and energized by such a frenzy of activity and natural buzz. The marks on my page as I asked the question 'How do you touch me?' were vibrant, quite psychedelic and I was so stunned with the vibrancy and beauty that the only way to express my amazement was by writing the word 'WOW'.

As this next story illustrates, when they mean business, plants have a powerful way of getting our attention. On our market stall one busy Saturday afternoon in Halifax, Nova Scotia, our flowers were mostly sold out so I decided to display a few bottles of freshly made flower essences. I didn't normally do so, but on this particular afternoon it just felt like the right thing to do. I hadn't even got out the explanatory leaflets when a young woman appeared out of nowhere and scooped up the red clover flower essence. 'She needs this, I know she does,' she said to her partner, not even reading the label. She did then pause to ask me what it was and what it was for. I explained and she nodded in agreement, obviously knowing it really was exactly what her friend needed.

After her visit I put away the essences; it didn't seem necessary to have them displayed any more, red clover needed to reach out to someone and had done her part. What caused this woman to stop by my table? I will never know for sure, but this type of instinct and sensitivity to plants and their particular vibration is a skill that, with practice, you can attune yourself to.

Sensory Exploration: Observation

'And above all, watch with glittering eyes the whole
world around you because the greatest secrets
are always hidden in the most unlikely places.
Those who don't believe in magic will never find it.'
— **ROALD DAHL,** *The Minpins*

It might seem pretty obvious that you should begin developing your relationships with plants by observing them in their natural habitat and I know you are dying to get into something much more mysterious and exciting – but bear with me, this is important stuff.

We are actually not as observant as we think we are. Our ego makes all sorts of prejudgments when we approach plants, for example, assuming it knows what a rose looks like, or a dandelion. In fact if I asked you to draw on paper now a rose or a dandelion you would probably come up with a very standard but acceptable drawing that in many ways does resemble a rose or a dandelion. However, with these assumptions we are missing the magic.

This is especially true when we are hanging out with plants that we are already familiar with, like the old favourites rose and dandelion. In the case of the rose, for example, our eyes and our brain are primed to look for those aspects that we are already familiar with and are expecting to find – like thorns and colourful petals arranged in a familiar shape. So this might be all we see; we might miss the caterpillar that is taking a snooze on the plant or overlook the exquisite way the petals unfold.

If we just take a glance at a plant, we won't see the intricacies at work. We need to consider each plant as an expression of consciousness that is communicating with us. Plants do this through colour, shape, smell, size, taste, vibration to name but a few. To get to know a plant fully we need to spend time in its presence, hang out with it in its home, really observe how it grows and what grows around it. We can also look at what other animals it may harbour, how it forms itself as it grows, where there might be patterns and what the colours are. We can learn a lot by simply being observant of the way that the plant grows and expresses itself as an expression of consciousness.

How observant are you of the vital nature of the plants that grow around you?

Observation Exercises

EXERCISE 1 Open Your Eyes

1. Sit with your chosen plant and greet the plant with a smile and a hello. Ask yourself 'How do you touch me?' as detailed earlier and take out a small piece of paper and coloured pens. Spend five minutes doodling what you think you see. Don't focus on making an accurate drawing; it's only meant to be a colourful representation of how the plant touches you. At the end of the five minutes put this to one side.
2. Now open your eyes and your heart. Closely observe the plant that you see growing in front of you and make notes about what you see.
3. Begin by introducing yourself. It may help you to refer to the Plant Connection Checklist in the appendix.
4. You can use the Plant Observation table that follows on pages 72–73 to remind you what you are looking for. However, don't just use the questions like a tick list; what is most important is your interaction with the plant. If you are familiar with this plant already then put aside all that you think you know and start fresh. If this plant is new to you then, after you have completed the exercise, look it up in a local plant guide and identify it properly.

Plant Observation Sheet	
Plant Name	**General Observations**
Plant size (absolute, and also in relation to others growing nearby) and form	
Location: e.g., sun/shade, type of area/soil	
Location in relation to other plants or animals	
Is the plant isolated or are there others of the same species nearby?	
What does the area where the plant is growing feel like?	
Stage of growth: i.e., in bud/flower/ seed – is this in keeping with other plants in the area?	
How is the plant growing?– spreading/upright/twisted/cramped	
General appearance: e.g., healthy/ bug-eaten, happy/strong/weak?	
What attracted you to the plant?	

Plant Observation Sheet	
Plant Name	General Observations
Favourite feature of the plant and reasons why	
What is the first thought that comes into your mind when you see this plant (your first impression)?	
If the plant was trying to tell you something what might it say?	
Does the plant seem friendly?	
How do you feel about the plant? Where do you feel this in your body?	
What part of the body/mind or which ailment do you feel this plant has an affinity for?	
Colour – does this plant have a special colour or bring to mind any colours or patterns?	
Without touching it, how does it look like it will feel?	
Other sensations/feelings/ observations/patterns	

Take photos of the plant if you like to help you build up another form of identification.

If it feels appropriate here to explore your senses of touch, smell and taste then ask permission to do so and, if you feel like the response is open and welcoming, then dive right in. For further exercises to develop these senses with plants keep reading.

Always finish by saying thank you, thank you, thank you, and presenting an appropriate offering, as discussed in Chapter 5.

EXERCISE 2 Describing the Plant

After you have completed the exercise above, try this exercise later the same day.

Put away your notes and see what you can remember about the plant. If you have access to a voice recorder (maybe on your phone or tablet), record yourself describing each aspect of the plant as you can remember it. Imagine you are building up a mental picture of this plant for someone who has never come across it before.

When you are satisfied with your description, revisit the plant and play back the recording to yourself while you are in front of it. Notice which features you have missed. Do these feel important to you now?

EXERCISE 3 Expressing the Plant with Colour and Pattern

Please don't panic about this exercise, or ignore it, if you are nervous about drawing or using colour. Think of it as just another exercise to hone your observation skills. The idea is not to produce a work of art but simply to create marks on the page that for you represent aspects of the plant you have selected. I really encourage you to give this a go. You may find that you don't draw the whole plant but instead select a leaf, a texture, shape, burst of colour or even words that come to mind when you are in front of it.

Gather your tools for this mission: pad of paper, colour pens, pencils, paints or pastels – whatever you have handy. Remember also to have with you an appropriate offering.

Hold your intention in your heart and tune in to your personal feelings about the exercise. Note down how you are feeling (use the questions from the earlier self-awareness check-in exercise if they work for you).

Return to a plant that you have previously closely observed (remember your courtesy; greet the plant and let it know your intention). Then put your art critic aside, start breathing into your heart and allow your creativity to flow. Consider all the details that are before you, rather than making marks based on your preconceptions. Observe the plant closely for as long as you need and, when you are ready, get out your paper and start making marks to represent the plant on the page in front of you. Take as long as you like to do this; really let yourself go and tune in. Get lost in the plant and the page.

I have found myself before with purple squirls all over my page to represent rosemary, blue and yellow clouds coming from willow and sad, angry poems from a particular maple tree. These images and words are not for show, they are for your personal plant journey. Try not to judge them!

When you feel you have played enough with colour and pattern, give thanks to the plant, make sure you give your offering and leave it.

Back inside, review the images, colours, patterns or words that you have expressed on paper. Does anything surprise you? Does this add to your knowledge of the plant?

The Doctrine of Signatures

'It's not what you look at that matters, it's what you see.'

— HENRY DAVID THOREAU

The doctrine of signatures was a method of identifying plants and the diseases they would treat used by herbalists as far back as the Middle Ages. In simple terms, the basis of the doctrine of signatures is that parts of plants that look like a part of the body can be used to treat that part's ailments.

For example, eyebright, a plant whose flower looks like bright blue eyes, was used to treat eye diseases. The use of eyebright for this purpose was particularly common in the 1700s and it is still used as a remedy today.

This belief acquired its name after the publication in 1621 of a book by the German mystic Jacob Boehme called *The Signature of All Things*. The Swiss physician Paracelsus, an important advocate of the doctrine, stated that 'Nature marks each growth… according to its curative benefit.'

Similarly, the contemporary English botanist William Cole believed that 'the mercy of God… maketh… Herbes for the use of men, and hath… given them particular Signatures, whereby a man may read… the use of them.'

Due to the science-driven attitude of today, the doctrine of signatures is not now commonly referred to, and is belittled by some as 'magical thinking'. So get magical for a moment – imagine that plants are signposts for us. Imagine that through their form and growth pattern, plants can provide us with a way to stay healthy.

There are several types of plant signature. A plant's environmental niche refers to where a plant likes to grow, and indicates its affinity to hot, cold, damp or dry conditions. Traditional Chinese medicine categorizes human ailments in this way; for example, think of a dry cough and then think of a heavy chesty cough that produces lots of mucus – both are coughs but totally different. Plants that grow in water or close by tend to be allied with the balance of water in the body and thus are used to treat the kidneys, which act as our body's filter system.

Shape is another important plant signature. For example, large-leaved plants like elecampane, burdock, comfrey and mullein transpire lots of water through their leaves; this action can be thought of as corresponding to human perspiration and respiration, which allies these plants with the skin and lungs. Colour is also a key signature, with burgundy red often being associated with blood conditions and bright red with cooling heat and easing blood congestion; think of rosehips and hawthorn berries.

So while you are observing your plants, be open to these signatures. Open up your heart and your imagination. Let yourself loose with the amazing green being in front of you – what might it be willing to show you through its physical form or location?

Sensory Exploration: Touch and Texture

If you've completed any of the observation exercises so far, you've no doubt discovered how hard it is to observe a plant without reaching out to touch it. This is a natural instinct and we have been doing it since we were infants; touching is how we learn about texture. Plants have amazing textures, from the thick, furry, soft leaves of lamb's ear for example to the spiky thorns of a bramble. Touching plants stimulates in them an automatic response, which may be as subtle as a series of biochemical changes that help protect the plant or a very obvious mechanical action like the Venus flytrap snapping shut around its prey.

Fortunately plants often enjoy being stroked (like humans!), so this is your invitation to reach out and get up close, personal and tactile.

EXERCISE Exploring Touch

After you have spent time observing a plant, and if it feels appropriate, ask permission and reach out and touch it. Make notes on how the plant feels and how you sense it reacting to your touch.

Touch the stem, leaves (both sides), the flowers/seed or bud and notice how different they are. They may be dry, scratchy, soft, hairy, sharp, smooth, finely haired or toothed. Does the plant feel cool or warm? Dry or moist?

Do you sense that the plant enjoys being touched in certain areas and not others?

If it feels right then ask either mentally or out loud if it would be OK for you to pick a flower or leaf. Pause and listen for a response. Sense into the plant and breathe into your heart. If you receive a response that feels positive then go ahead and pick a leaf or flower.

Taking this in your hand, explore how it feels when it is placed over different areas of your body – start at your bare feet, then touch the plant to various parts of your body, maybe your belly, forearms, shoulders, heart, face, forehead and crown.

Give thanks to the plant. Take the part you've picked with you. You may wish to carry it with you, place it in water in your home, give it to someone or press it to keep as a record.

EXERCISE Feeling the Earth

The earth represents the nourishment and support that we all need, physically, emotionally and spiritually. She feeds our flesh, our minds and our souls; and yet how often do we really pause and honour the earth for all that she provides? Before you begin this exercise reflect on who you nourish and support in life. Are you nourished and supported in the way that you need? Do you have the support you need in your life right now?

You can use this hands-on exercise to really feel into the earth and make a connection through physical touch. When the time is right allow yourself the simple pleasure of kicking off your shoes and walking barefoot on the grass. Enjoy the fresh feeling as the soft grass slips between your toes and bends beneath your feet. Take the opportunity touch the earth; find some bare soil and for a moment just observe how it looks. Note how you think it is going to feel. Will it be soft or coarse? Warm or cold? Damp or dry? What is it made up of in this spot – does it contain sand, clay, small stones, dead matter?

When you are ready to experience the texture and temperature, plunge your hands into the earth's soil. Do this mindfully and as you work the soil through your fingers simply breathe and listen. Allow your body to relax and soften. Observe what thoughts and feelings come up for you. Try not to analyze; simply observe and let them gather. Does it give you pleasure to have dirt under your fingernails or do you feel unclean and uncomfortable? Personally I have some days when I can't bear the thought of getting covered in soil and yet other times I can spend all day getting dirt embedded deeply under my nails, in my hair, practically everywhere.

Talk to the earth and ask for support and nourishment where you need it right now in your life. Envisage the earth taking away negative energy and experiences that you are no longer in need of and are ready to give up. Focus on your heart space and allow your body to receive gifts from the earth. Be still and see what comes. When you feel ready, give thanks.

Take a look at the dirt on your hands. What feelings does it bring up? Do you feel unclean or do you feel connected? Think back to when you were a child; do you have memories of playing with soil or sand and water? (Is this something you were allowed to do?) Did it bring you joy or repulse you? As young children we are naturally curious and learn through touch. We don't often show the concern for dirt or discomfort in nature that an adult may perceive. Your attitude now will depend on how you experienced connecting to nature in this way as a child, but it can change over time. Allow yourself to reawaken and evaluate how you feel now.

Earth, Teach Me to Remember

Earth teach me stillness
as the grasses are stilled with light.
Earth teach me suffering
as old stones suffer with memory.

Earth teach me humility
as blossoms are humble with beginning.
Earth teach me caring
as the mother who secures her young.
Earth teach me courage
as the tree which stands alone.
Earth teach me limitation
as the ant which crawls on the ground.
Earth teach me freedom
as the eagle which soars in the sky.
Earth teach me resignation
as the leaves which die in the fall.
Earth teach me regeneration
as the seed which rises in the spring.
Earth teach me to forget myself
as melted snow forgets its life.
Earth teach me to remember kindness
as dry fields weep in the rain.

— JOHN YELLOW LARK,
Lakota Chief

EXERCISE Herbal Bathing

After all this playing in the mud, you might enjoy treating yourself to a herbal bath. Our bodies can absorb a great number of the medicinal components of plants through our skin. In the 1940s and 50s, French herbalist Maurice Mességué primarily used hand and foot baths to administer herbal remedies.

Run a warm bath and add a handful of rose petals, chamomile flowers or lavender flowers for a feeling of nourishment and relaxation. While you are bathing, rub the flowers and petals into your skin to experience the touch of these plants and enjoy their fragrance.

If you don't have access to herbs or petals, make a strong infusion of chamomile tea and add this to your bath. You can also experiment with different essential oils added to a carrier oil or bath salts for use in your bath.

MEDITATION Walking Meditation

This exercise involves directing your full attention to the action of walking, rather than being absorbed in your thoughts. Try it barefoot to really connect with the earth beneath your feet.

The idea of a walking meditation is not the destination; you are not focusing on where you are going. You are simply focusing on the sensation of walking as your feet, legs and whole body moves, and the awareness of your breathing as you are walking.

The key is to be present in every step, feeling your feet touch the earth, sensing the movement and all the other shifts that occur in your body and breath as you walk. Keep your gaze focused slightly in front of you at a distance of about a metre.

Try out the walking meditation in a small area between five and ten metres. A path to tread backwards and forwards is ideal so that you don't have to think about where you are going. Give yourself 10 to 15 minutes for this exercise.

Practise walking mindfully for a few minutes and then reduce the speed of your pace by half. Walk in this way for five more minutes and then reduce the speed of your pace by half again. Walk in this way for a further five minutes or so. Notice where your balance is, notice which parts of your feet touch the ground. Carefully consider where you will place each step. Are you able to relax and slow to this new pace or does this exercise frustrate you?

Experiment at different times of the day and with shoes on and without to experience the difference.

Sensory Exploration: Smell

Plants produce fragrances to attract pollinators and also to deter predators. Compare the sweet, attractive, delicious aromas of honey to a harsh and bitter stink that burns your nose – yuck! Amazingly, flowers identical in colour and shape can have slightly different scents, due to the complex combination of volatile compounds and their interactions. Species pollinated by bees and flies will generally carry sweet scents, whereas those pollinated by beetles will generally carry strong musty, spicy or fruity odours.

In humans, fragrance triggers emotional responses and memories due to the way that we process smell in our brains. Sometimes a perfume, the scent of a flower or something cooking in the oven can take us right back to our childhood. What fragrances trigger memories for you? I remember visiting my family home one spring during my university holidays and picking armfuls of daffodils from the back garden. I arranged them in vases all over the house and each time you entered a room the scent was overpowering. Both my mother and myself have never forgotten that weekend and every spring when I smell the daffodils, the sweet fragrance takes me right back there.

When we ran our flower farm my partner and I would, every year, grow sweet peas. We are total suckers for their beautiful old-fashioned scent and glorious range of colours and we figured others would be too. So, despite the hard work of having to tie them up and harvest them regularly, we never failed to produce sweet peas (we still do so at home!) each year. Every week we had them on the market stall, the sweet peas received the same reaction – without fail someone would come up to the table exclaiming with joy, 'Wow, I love sweet peas, the smell reminds me of my grandma…' and then a story would follow.

It brings joy to my heart to think of how many fond memories of our grandparents who grew sweet peas are out there in the world. I also wonder, wistfully, what will our grandchildren remember us for?

As well as evoking beautiful memories, the smell produced by a plant can also act as a vehicle for our personal healing. Before seeing one of my clients for treatment, as was customary for me I went for a walk to contemplate her visit. As I passed several pines I had the sense that these big and beautiful trees needed to be involved somehow. I spent a moment breathing with the trees and asked permission to cut a small branch, letting the trees know of my intention, then placed the branch in water in my treatment room, in lieu of a vase of flowers.

During the treatment, there was a lot of energy movement and release; the client had been suffering from grief and was carrying a lot of stagnant energy. I felt drawn to take the pine and place it on certain areas of the client's body, focusing especially on the heart. Then to finish the treatment I took bunches of the needles and crumpled them between my fingers. This released the gorgeous scent of pine throughout the room and into my client's energy field. I let the pine needles fall onto my client, scattering them from her head to her feet. This really seemed to perk up and re-energize my client and, during the feedback session afterwards, she talked about how strong and wonderful she felt when she smelt the pine. It sounded like that was one of the highlights of her treatment. She was visibly relaxed and it looked like a burden had been lifted. She then started telling me how lately she had been looking at a large pine in her garden and it had been in her thoughts a lot. It's clear to me that pine had been trying to get her attention in some way because it knew it was the medicine that she needed; and through the treatment with me, and its glorious and unique fragrance, it succeeded. I suggested that she spend some time with the pine tree in her garden and be open to any more thoughts, feelings and ideas that might come her way.

Many of us will be familiar with the fragrances of plants like pine, lavender, lilies and roses, not to mention the highly aromatic culinary herbs like thyme, basil, mint, rosemary and sage. These aromatic plants are bold and easily make themselves known. One February I had spent several days interacting with rosemary because I had many plants in my house for the winter to protect them from the -19 Celsius temperatures outside. I was feeling a lot of companionship from the plants; they were giving me strength and warmth.

I went out one night to join a sweat to celebrate the festival of Imbolc with a group of local women. During the sweat, the atmosphere became magical, light and fun and we all felt the presence of the green world – it was opening its doors. The sweat lodge became filled with the scent of rosemary, even though none had been used on the hot rocks. I smiled to myself. Oh yes, rosemary, of course she is here. 'Hello Rosemary,' we all chorused, 'Welcome and thank you for your blessings.'

EXERCISE Scent of a Plant

After you have spent time observing a plant, exploring how it feels to touch it, lean in and search for the fragrance that the plant carries. Discover which parts carry the scent. Note down how it makes you react. Is it pleasant? Does it stir up any memories or associations? Does it lodge itself in any area of your body? Choose three words to describe it.

If it feels appropriate, ask permission to take a piece of the plant to accompany your day. Give thanks as always.

Essential Oils

We are very fortunate these days that we have so many varieties of plant essential oils available to us. (Please always purchase oils from reliable sources that are sustainably harvested and ethically produced.)

Using essential oils in a burner or diffuser is another really simple way of inviting the fragrance and spirit of a particular plant into your space. Whenever I use essential oils, I make sure to do a special prayer of thanks as the fragrance of the oil first touches me. In this honouring I am giving thanks to all of the plants that were used in the making of the essential oil.

To get to know particular plants in this way, through their fragrance, I suggest experimenting with a few oils individually through the following exercise.

EXERCISE **Exploring Essential Oils**

Get comfortable in your sacred space and be sure that you will not be disturbed.

Close your eyes and sit peacefully. Relax into your body and just land here, breathing deeply, at peace.

Turn your attention inside and slowly mentally do a sweep of your body to feel where you might be experiencing tension, discomfort, heaviness or other sensations.

Whenever you experience discomfort, send your breath to that place and as you exhale, release.

Continue this process until you have covered your entire body, then rest your attention back at your heart.

Breathe in and out another nine times at your heart, breathing in peace. Each time you breathe out try to open your heart and relax into the space a little more.

Open your eyes and place the essential oil in the burner or diffuser to start its action.

Return to your position, close your eyes and centre yourself once again.In your own way offer your thanks and gratitude to the many plants that were used to produce the oil you are using.

As the scent of the oil flows through the air, notice your initial sensation as it hits you.

In your mind's eye greet the plant and open your heart, inviting the plant to be with you.

Breathe here for as long as you need, focusing your attention on your heart and with each breath allowing the scent and the spirit of the plant to enter more deeply into your body.

Observe the sensations in your body.

Observe the thoughts, memories, feelings that come into your mind.

Notice if there is a particular part of your body that wants to attract the plant, or maybe wants to push the plant away; notice the location of resistance and willingness, notice tension and openness.

Notice if any colours or patterns are coming to mind.

Notice if any words or shapes are forming.

See what comes, feel into what is, breathe effortlessly.

When you are ready, give thanks to the plant and finish your meditation.

Open your eyes and stop the diffuser or extinguish the burner.

The scent of the plant will linger with you. Stay in this place with your journal and start to write, draw, colour on paper or whatever comes to mind, whatever wants to flow. Note down your feelings and how you are feeling in your body.

This exercise can be repeated with the same essential oil again and again to invite the plant to go deeper with you. You can try it with different intentions or with questions that are on your mind and see what comes. Also experiment with different essential oils and notice how the experiences differ; note which qualities the different oils have and which appeal to you more.

EXERCISE Combining Touch and Smell Blindfold

With a partner, decide who is going to go first and get the first person to put on a blindfold or scarf to cover their eyes. The other person should take them around the garden to various plants; at each one the blindfolded person can spend time exploring the plant with their hands and then lean in to smell it. At each plant make sure you both introduce yourselves, explain what you are doing and express your gratitude with an offering of thanks. Make sure you experiment with different plants and switch roles.

Sensory Exploration: Taste

Thanks to the way that our brain works, taste, like our sense of smell, is linked to our emotions; the senses of smell and taste are also linked to each other. For example, our mouths water when we smell bread baking in the oven.

Our taste buds have evolved over time to help us survive by identifying the difference between poisonous food and nutritious food. The Ayurvedic way of working with herbs identifies six basic qualities of taste, known as Rasa in Sanskrit: sweet, sour, salty, bitter, pungent and astringent. Think of honey, lemons, olives, coffee, garlic and cranberries. We are all familiar with the hot sensation of spicy too, but in theory this is actually not a taste but a pain response!

These different tastes can help us to understand more about the physical qualities and chemical properties of a plant and the effect it may have on the body. If we are working with medicinal plants we can use this information when formulating a herbal preparation – for example a bitter plant would not be suitable for a tea.

Resist the urge to nibble every plant you meet! My advice is not to go ahead and break off a tiny piece of the plant to put in your mouth until you have identified it as being non-poisonous. When experimenting with the taste of plants, always approach with caution and loving respect. Don't just dive in there and grab a handful of leaves. As in the previous exercises, say hello, hold the intention in your heart to get to know the plant better and ask for permission. Pause before you break off a piece of the plant to sample. If you don't feel that there is any opening towards you doing this, then leave it alone.

EXERCISE Exploring Taste

If you feel that the plant is willing for you to taste it and you have identified it as safe, then take a small piece of the leaf or seed and place it on your tongue. If at any point you have a prickly sensation or anything else that feels odd, spit it out!

Otherwise proceed to hold the plant on your tongue and note and observe the taste and the sensations in your body.

Try to summarize the plant's taste with a phrase or a word. Does this give you an indication of its personality? As always, be sure to thank the plant when you finish.

If you wish to take more of the plant with you, to prepare an infusion at home for example, then simply ask and respond accordingly. When wild harvesting always make sure that you don't decimate one particular plant, especially if that is the only one in the area. If you only encounter one plant then leave it alone. If you find an area with an abundance of the same plants then harvest a little from each of them. Be selective when wild harvesting, you are looking for a healthy specimen, don't select plants growing at the roadside or those which have been eaten by insects.

EXERCISE Exploring Taste and Smell Together

Make a strong herbal infusion of your choice, such as nettle or fennel. If you don't have access to fresh or dry herbs then use several herbal tea bags to make your brew, or make a fresh ginger infusion by grating a large tablespoon of fresh ginger into a cup of hot water. Be sure to cover the top of your mug and leave for at least 20 minutes to fully infuse. Take your infusion into your sacred space and sit quietly; centre yourself and breathe calmly so you can be fully present to meet the plant.

Take three deep breaths and hold in your heart your intention to meet this plant.

Start by holding the brew in your hands and just observe the colour of the liquid.

Next, bring the cup close up to your face and inhale the aroma. Spend at least five minutes on this. As the aroma touches your nose open up all of your senses; open your heart and invite the plant into your body. Be aware of any thoughts and feelings that the aroma brings up for you. How would you describe it in one word? Does this give you an indication of the plant's personality? Do you feel your body and soul opening to it or withdrawing?

As you inhale the aroma from the infusion does it travel anywhere in your body?

After at least another five minutes, when you feel ready, take a sip of the infusion. Notice your first impression of the taste; is it how you expected? Warm/cool, bitter/sweet, sharp or tangy? Where does it travel to in your body? Does it evoke certain memories or emotions? How do you feel about this plant? Does your body welcome it or is it withdrawing? Do you wish to drink more of the infusion?

Sit quietly and mindfully drink the infusion, focusing on inviting the plant into your body. Check in with yourself to note how you are feeling physically, intellectually, emotionally and spiritually. Does this plant merit further investigation for you right now?

Plant Diets

Ceremonial plant dieting is a traditional way of honouring a plant to connect deeply with its wisdom and meet its spirit for healing. Plant diets are ancient and have mostly been forgotten by our Western culture, but they are still practised in indigenous cultures as a powerful tool for transformation and healing. You may associate plant diets with powerful psychoactive plants and brews (ayahuasca, for example) that promote visionary experiences.

However, in their most simple form plant diets can be carried out with local plants that are sustainable and easily accessible. A plant diet might consist of you ingesting the plant each day as a tea or as a juice for an entire moon cycle, or even dieting on solely a chosen plant for one or two days as part of a ceremony. Ingesting plants in this way with honour, respect and ritual helps us to form a closer bond and expand our consciousness to meet the spirit of the plant in a new and focused way. Consider it a plant initiation. If you love plants it can be highly pleasurable spending some intimate one-to-one time with one of your friends.

A plant diet requires planning and preparation both beforehand and afterwards. After a plant diet or ceremony, you must be gentle with yourself; you may have experienced a huge transformation, so allow yourself time and space to integrate your experiences. You may like to continue working with the plant, or taking it as an essence or infusion, or simply sitting with it in meditation for continued support and companionship. Offer your prayers and blessings and, as always, your gratitude.

In the next chapter we will discuss ceremony further, but for now experiment with some of the following.

- Replace coffee with herbal teas, go meat-free and try to include as many vegetables and fruits as you can in your diet.
- Explore the wild foods that can be foraged in your area.
- Get experimental with your cooking and food preparation. For new flavours add herbs and edible flowers to your everyday dishes. For example, add handfuls of mixed herbs to a plain omelette or pizza and nasturtium, borage or calendula flowers to your salads.

- Notice which foods and flavours dominate your food palate (normally this is sweet and salty). Try to increase the quantity of astringent, sour, pungent or bitter food in your diet.
- Consider your buying choices. Are you able to buy organic or from local growers?

The first plant diet I did at home was for 48 hours, with yarrow. This wasn't part of a huge ceremony; it was just myself and the plant. I wanted to get to know a plant a little better and Yarrow seemed willing.

I carried out the diet at home with a group of plants close by so that I could visit them as part of the ceremony and had easy access to the plant material. I dieted on yarrow infusion, drinking it warm the first day and cold the next. I also ate light salads to keep me going and was guided to break the fast with red berries. Over the 48 hours I carried out many meditations and journeys to meet the spirit of yarrow. I also spent time physically with the plant, drawing, writing poetry, singing and dancing; held a fire ceremony in the evening; and enjoyed a herbal bath with yarrow blossoms.

The experience was both thrilling and enlightening. I received many messages, stories and wisdom from this feathery, strong and powerful plant. What is especially interesting is that I was at the time suffering from stagnation; I wasn't moving forward with many of my projects and was stuck in a very dull routine. After the plant diet, I found myself with fire in my belly, fresh wind in my sails and enthusiasm for my projects. I put this down entirely to the medicine of yarrow, which is such a powerful mover and shaker. I am forever grateful.

This experience has also brought me closer to the plant; yarrow has always been a special ally for me and since this plant diet, even more so. I feel that we now have an even deeper understanding and respect for each other. I highly recommend this type of experience for getting to know a plant on a different level.

Think of how intense it would be to spend 24 hours with one human, absorbing not only their energy but their physical properties as well! It can be interesting to experiment with a plant in a one-to-one situation, but it is also so rewarding to do it as part of a group, so maybe get together with some friends and see where that takes you.

Sensory Exploration: Listening

It might seem a little unusual to include our sense of hearing, when we generally consider plants to be silent beings, but put your cynicism aside and open up to this possibility. Not only can plants produce sound themselves but they also make sound as the wind and rain weave through their foliage.

Music of the Plants

For over thirty years the community of Damanhur in Italy has been researching communication with the plant world. As part of this research, they have created a device that when clipped on to a plant's leaves and roots is able to read the electromagnetic variations that occur and turn them into sounds and movement. The music produced varies based on the response of the plant to stimuli in the environment. What's more, the plants seem to enjoy the sounds and will learn to produce them themselves. As well as live concerts combining plant music with human singing, there are CDs available, so you can investigate further if this interests you.

Plants, just like humans, have personalities and preferences. I find that some really enjoy music, being sung to or read to. Some plants respond to a drum and others seem to find that sound too harsh and prefer a gentler sound, like that of a rattle.

All plants seem to both enjoy and inspire song. During plant ceremonies curanderos of the Amazon, together with participants, will chant, sing and hum specific icaros (sacred power songs) to guide the ceremony. The icaros call to the spirits of the plants to deliver their strength and medicine for healing, cleansing, protection or whatever is needed.

I certainly find song to be one of the main channels of communication between myself and plants. This started in Nova Scotia when I was harvesting flowers at the farm, and these days I still can't seem to stop myself from singing if I am in the garden or out walking the dog. They are simple songs of blessing or wordless sounds that speak out from somewhere deep inside as well as from the trees and plants that surround me, and seem to shift the atmosphere around me.

EXERCISE **Asking a Plant for Song**

> Next time you are with a plant, consider – if it were to carry a sound what might that be?

Does the plant inspire a song in you? Ask it for a song and see what comes. Sit quietly, opening up your heart and breathing through your heart space. Allow yourself to receive from the plant. You may find you begin to gently sway or start tapping your fingers. Spend some time with this and see where it takes you.

Your song may turn into a dance; if so, let yourself move with the plant and allow what needs to move through you to do so. Have fun and enjoy.

As always, give gratitude.

EXERCISE Opening Your Ears to Nature

Next time you are out in your favourite place in nature, take a seat and close your eyes. Relax into your position and take a few deep breaths with long exhalations to get yourself fully present and grounded in the moment. Steady your breathing and, keeping your eyes closed, begin to open your ears to the sounds that surround you. You will notice the obvious sounds at first; the loudest and those that are nearest or the most annoying or unnatural, like planes flying overhead.

Be patient and allow your sense of listening to go beyond these. Sink into your sense of hearing, listening for the faintest sounds, the sweetest sounds, those that are unusual or sporadic and distant. Are the sounds natural, from creatures or the elements like water or wind? Or are they unnatural, man-made, machine-generated? Notice which sounds you can pick up that tell you what is present in the air around you today. What do the sounds tell you about the energy of the day, time of day or time of year? How do those sounds make you feel? Are there sounds that are more pleasant than others? Which are those sounds that you lean into?

This can be a difficult exercise because we are often unaccustomed to listening for soft, unobvious sounds. Music and sound play such an important role in many people's lives, developing your sense of hearing to attune to the subtle sounds of nature will surprise you.

EXERCISE Full Body Immersion

If you haven't already, take it right from the top and let a plant choose you, sit with it, observe, touch, smell, taste and listen. Take your time – this really could take all day!

EXERCISE Forest Bathing

The Japanese have come up with a gentle healing therapy called Shinrin-Yoku, which translates as 'forest bathing'. In the 1980s the practice became a key part of their preventative healthcare system. Studies have shown a wide array of physiological and psychological health benefits including reduced stress, enhanced immune response, improved moods and sharper cognition. The US-based Association of Nature and Forest Therapy is establishing a global network of trained Forest Therapy guides and aims to integrate the practice of forest therapy into healthcare systems.

To explore the benefits of this kind of therapy, take yourself to a woodland or a wooded area of your local park and try it for yourself. The Woodland Trust in the UK has a wood search facility on their website to help you easily discover woodland that is local to you. If you feel vulnerable heading out alone, then join forces with a friend or group of friends and always makes sure you have told someone where you are heading.

1. As you enter the woods, take a few deep breaths and mentally leave your everyday life behind. Also let go of any goals or expectations of the exercise. Let yourself wander aimlessly, allowing your body to take you wherever it wants.

2. From time to time take a pause; look more closely at a leaf that is in your path or feel the sensation of the ground beneath your feet.

3. If you can find a suitable spot, take a seat and listen to the sounds of the woodland around you. Notice how the birds and other wildlife react to your presence and become used to you.

4. When you feel ready, wander back to where you began your journey. Mentally give thanks to the woodland for your experience. Make any notes in your journal of your experience, what stood out for you and how it made you feel.

During a lunchtime dog walk in my local woods just before the winter solstice I became aware of a palpable difference in the atmosphere around me. Though the trees were completely still there was a movement, an aliveness and brightness that seemed to glow through the bare winter branches. As I stepped further along the path I felt a warm ball of light hit me right in the heart and then spread out through me like a bubble expanding to include me. It was as if I had somehow stepped through a membrane or portal into a liminal space of wonder and magic. I felt my heart expand and my pace slow down. I began to feel mischievous and childlike. I became filled with a sense of wonder that was a far cry from the head-chatter that had been bothering me at the start of my walk. A song came through me with a merry tune and accompanied me for the rest of my walk. It was only when I left the woods and was greeted by the noise of the traffic and 'real world' once again that I noticed they had both gone. The warmth in my heart, however, stayed with me for the rest of the day.

The words that came were:

I feel blessed
I feel true
I feel blessed
That I am a part of you.

Chapter Summary

This chapter demonstrates the information that is easily accessible and available to us from plants that grow locally, as well as the fun that you can have when you open up all of your physical senses to the plant kingdom.

I hope you have enjoyed the various exercises in this chapter and are already feeling a little closer to your green allies.

KEY POINTS

- Make an effort to develop your peripheral vision and pay attention to which plants might be trying to get your attention.
- Be fully present when you are working with plants and leave what you think you know aside.
- Take the time to fully observe a plant in its habitat.
- With permission, touch, smell and taste the plant (only taste if you can positively identify the plant as non-poisonous).
- Don't forget your ears; open up to the stillness of a forest or particular plant – you never know what music you will be blessed with.

In the next chapter we will build on the strengths of your physical senses and get more practically involved in the life of a plant to give you a deeper understanding of and interaction with plants as conscious beings.

Hands-on Interaction:
Plants for Pleasure,
Nourishment and Beauty

One of the reasons that my awakening to plant consciousness came so intensely is because most of the plants I spent time with were my babies that I had nurtured from seed. All of the annual flowers that we grew started as tiny seeds, often no larger than pinheads, that my partner and I lovingly and laboriously sowed into compost. After that came the watering, then transplanting into larger pots, hardening off the plants after they had been in the greenhouse and, finally, transplanting them into the field. As any gardener knows, the care and attention did not stop there.

We visited our plants each day, checking for pests such as rodents, deer, birds and bugs, sun damage, waterlogging, frost or wind damage. I was totally immersed in each phase of the life of these beautiful plants, right from their emergence as tiny seedlings to their gorgeous blooming, which led to harvesting, admiring their beauty, sharing it with others and watching them go to seed and then finally come to their end as the winter frost hit. I was present for the full life cycle of the annuals and was also companion to many biennials, perennials, shrubs and trees that we planted on the property or that were already growing there when we arrived. This constant presence was the key to me becoming accustomed to the vibrations of the plants that grew around me and meant that I was often completely immersed in their energy fields so I understood what they were communicating and what they needed, and was able to communicate back.

Get Growing

If you don't already, then start growing something green and experience the plant life cycle for yourself. Even if you don't have the space to germinate seeds at home, why not start by planting some bulbs in the autumn or buying some transplants (small plants to replant at home) from a garden centre in the spring? These days you can purchase a wonderful variety of ornamentals and edibles like tomato plants, which you can grow in pots to place on a small balcony or terrace. You don't need to have acres of space or any prior knowledge of plants. Even if you just have one plant that you look after on your windowsill, nurture and grow with, by being present in your heart space with the plant you will feel a transformation in yourself and develop a wonderful bond with your plant.

I simply adore growing flowers because they bring so much joy, not only to me and my partner but to anyone visiting my garden or receiving a bunch of colourful blooms. I could meditate on a flower for ages; they are so intricate and beautiful. Choose something that you love. Turn up at a garden centre with the intention in mind that you have come to pick up a plant or two to take home and get to know, and see what happens. Do beware though – plants are charismatic and highly appealing and make it very easy to overspend at the garden centre!

Easy flowers for growing in the UK

- Bulbs (planted in the autumn): hyacinth, daffodil, tulip, lily, allium, muscari and crocus.
- Violas and pansies
- Sweet peas
- Calendula
- Field poppies
- Snapdragons
- Sunflowers
- Nasturtiums

Great garden herbs for cooking and herbal tea for growing in the UK

- Chamomile – charming annual and self-seeds.
- All the mints – peppermint, spearmint, chocolate mint, ginger mint etc.
- Thyme – many varieties including lemon thyme.
- Rosemary – my favourite companion in the garden.
- Sage – many varieties, all beautiful and flavoursome in teas.
- Lemon balm – fabulous fragrance and lovely as a relaxing infusion.

- Coriander – an easy annual to grow from seed and will reseed and come again the next year if the plant is left to go to seed.
- Basil – a delicious annual that pairs well with tomatoes. It needs plenty of warmth and sun to grow so, if you are not blessed with that at home, purchase small plants from your local supermarket and buy more as you need.

Other garden must-haves: it's best not to get me started on all the edible ones, so I'll just say that lavender and roses are two plants that I simply can't live without because of their beauty, exquisite fragrance and general easygoing nature. The list of plants, herbs, trees and flowers that are close to my heart is endless. For you it will be the same. Over and over I hear clients saying they are 'no good with plants', but I believe that's just a case of not finding the right plant at the right time in life. If that has been your experience then I urge you to try again.

If you have access to an outside terrace or garden, spend time in that space quietly tuning in and opening up your senses. Get the feel of the place before deciding what to plant. Leave a wild area untouched so that the spirit of nature can thrive without interference.

When planting, prepare the area in a sacred and loving way with purpose and intention. Whisper your prayers for your planting and talk to the land so it knows what is to be planted there and what its purpose is. When planting out seeds and transplants, hold them tenderly in your hands, sending them your love, intentions for healthy growth and well wishes.

Over the course of the growing season, hang out with your plants outside, observe their different stages of growth, their energy and how they appear to interact with other plants and wildlife in the garden.

If you have a house plant, experiment by moving it to different locations in your home and observing any changes that you notice in its appearance, growth pattern and sense of energy.

Notice how you feel when you are spending time with your plants. Perhaps you have a favourite stage of growth or a favourite plant that you particularly like to spend time with. You may feel that you want to select a plant to spend time with every day for an entire moon cycle. When watering your plants say short prayers and blessings to the water and also to the plants themselves. Sing your plants songs, tell them your story, appreciate their beauty and give them your love; you will soon see and feel the difference.

Creating Sacred Space

Calling in the directions to open the space and welcome helping spirits

Drumming to raise the energy

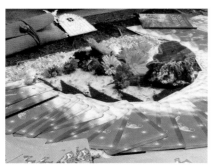

An altar with plant offerings

Cleansing space by burning herb bundles

Attuning to Plants

Opening your senses to nature, breathing and receiving

Cornflower meadow with blossoms ready to harvest

Expressing first impressions with colour

Connecting with a tree for support and grounding

Creating Essences, Oils and Tinctures

Talk to plants while you harvest, take them on a journey

Chop plant material to release its active components

Mugwort ready to be infused in oil

A mortar and pestle for tough roots, bark and seeds

Creating infused oil from Saint John's Wort flowers and buds

Fresh rose petals – a recipe for love

Edible flowers from the garden

Shamanic teacher Fotoula Adrimi shared with me a really beautiful Greek shamanic tradition from Thessaly, which is one of the many traditions that are passed down orally within a family. It's the custom of kissing the new growth of a plant as it appears. As a child, Fotoula watched her great-aunts carry out this tradition. Her father's tomatoes were the envy of the town! She has since adopted it too. It's a beautiful blessing to give to plants and really helps connect you to their vital essence.

As I have mentioned, when working with plants aim to be feeling your way from your heart space rather than thinking your way using your mental head space. This can be very challenging, especially when logic, reason or practicality is giving you reason to use a plant in a certain way and the whisper of your heart is giving you a different story.

In the first year of setting up our small farm, my partner and I experienced the push and pull of logic and feeling in a number of ways. There was an overwhelming number of urgent jobs both large and small that needed tending to. Although we had planned our planting schedule and field layout, time got the better of us and when it came to transplanting certain herbs and flowers, they simply had to go where there was room or suitable tilled land. The result was that many didn't survive the first winter, or by the time they did surface in the spring they were overcome by weeds and either impossible to locate or simply grew small and stunted.

But this was a good teaching from Mother Nature and we learned from the experience. In subsequent years and still now, whenever I have a new seedling to transplant or a new herb to add to my garden, I take a deep breath and, rather than make decisions from my head space, I get into my heart space.

Breathing deeply and focusing on my heart helps me connect and feel into the energy around the plants that I am with. I ask a question: 'Where would you like to go?', 'Where are you going to thrive for your good and for the good of the garden?', 'Who would like to go in this area next to the barn?', for example. I wait and see what feeling I am given in response. If nothing comes then I go ahead and get planting wherever I had in mind. However, more often than not, I will suddenly have a new idea that I hadn't previously thought of and take my plants over there, even though it may not seem that logical. I like to place the plant down in the chosen spot and see how it looks. So as well as see with my eyes, I will open up my heart and senses and 'feel' with my senses how it looks and feels in this spot. If all is well I will plant. If I can't seem to tune in to anything then I may decide not to plant on this day after all and wait for a while. So my advice for planting is, essentially, 'Be in your heart space rather than head space.'

Extract from a Druid Planting Prayer

... Though you are mighty you hurt no creature.
Though you sustain us with your breath, you will give up
your life to house and warm and teach us.
We give thanks for your blessing upon our lives
and upon our lands...

Making Plant Medicine

Start by using plants as much as possible in your diet, making wholesome food for your body and soul. If you have an interest in medicinal plants, experiment with easy-to-grow herbs like calendula, feverfew, chamomile, lemon balm, rosemary, thyme and varieties of mint. You may also be able to forage for local herbs such as St John's wort, nettle, comfrey, elder-flower, meadowsweet, plantain or dandelion. The easiest herbal medicines to make are infusions and infused oils; once you have mastered these you can progress to making simple medicinal syrups, salves and tinctures using a basic herbal for instruction.

Any medicines that you make from plants that you have gathered or even grown yourself will carry a much higher vibration and healing poten-tial than something that you have bought from a store and which may have been imported from overseas. I am addicted to good herbal books so I have recommended a few of my favourites in the bibliography.

Gardening with Ho'oponopono

Ho'oponopono is a Hawaiian practice for forgiveness that I often use in the garden. It comes in very handy when you are weeding, pruning, thin-ning, transplanting and harvesting plants. It's a very simple and heart-opening prayer to use, at any time, but it is especially useful in the garden. I find it particularly valuable when I have been really appreciating certain plants, like flowers that have bloomed or tomatoes that are ripe, and want to harvest them for food or to display in a vase. The prayer helps me ask for forgiveness and also removes any guilt I may feel about harvesting from the plant.

The prayer goes like this:

I am sorry
Please forgive me
I love you
Thank you

Creating Beauty

If you are lucky enough to have flowers in your garden, or foliage from bushes and trees, then enjoy playing with them and create something beautiful for yourself and for others. When we owned the flower farm, Friday was our favourite day of the week because this was the day that we made up all of the bouquets to take to the Saturday farmers' market. We would stand in the flower barn surrounded by blooms of all shapes and sizes, put the music on and get creative. It was such a joy to be surrounded by all that colour and those unique expressions of beauty.

We used to have many volunteer workers help us out on the farm and they would usually start the day very hesitant to work with the flowers; we would hear comments like 'Oh, I don't think I can arrange flowers.' I would always tell them that it really is impossible to make anything made of fresh cut flowers look terrible, because flowers are so incredibly beautiful (and I like to believe that I am right!). Without fail the volunteers would surprise themselves at how much they enjoyed arranging flowers into bouquets and how striking their floral creations were. Each bouquet always seemed to reflect the character of the person who had made it and every week we sold out.

Playing with flowers is such fun but sadly they are not viewed as a weekly home essential on the shopping list. I also know many vegetable growers and herbalists who don't grow flowers because they aren't 'useful', whereas in my view flowers, as bringers of joy, have the highest purpose of all. Fortunately there has been a growth in recent years across the UK and the US of smaller, local flower growers who have brought back the seasonal blooms of cottage gardens that are not normally stocked by traditional florists.

British florist Juliet Glaves reminds us 'There is no comparison between forced, farmed flowers and naturally grown ones, which are robust and beautifully imperfect.' The most satisfaction can be had when you can use flowers that are grown locally or those that you grow yourself; even if you buy a pot of sweet peas from the garden centre, these will grow all summer long if you put them against a wall to grow up, and will provide you with lovely flowers for cute posies. Find out about your local flower growers and get to know the seasonal varieties that grow well in your area.

One spring we grew so many hyacinths… I guess you could say we got a bit carried away. I ended up with so many bulbs in bloom and, rather than sell them, I had a better idea. A friend and her daughters had recently returned from a trip to India and I was seeing them that night for the first time since their return. I threaded the hyacinth flowers on to string to create a garland of flowers for each of them. When I saw them that evening I presented each one with her own beautifully scented 'lei' or garland of flowers to wear around their necks. They had tears in their eyes. It was such a beautiful moment.

I encourage you to have fun with flowers, petals, leaves and grasses. Create physical representations of natural wonder to adorn yourself, your friends and your home – with the plants' permission of course.

The next time you pass a florist let yourself get carried away by the blooms; step inside and buy flowers for a friend – and make sure you can be there in person when they receive them. Enjoy their reaction.

Seed Saving

On the farm we always used to grow heritage vegetables from heirloom seed that had been lovingly saved by generation after generation of growers. If you have been able to grow your own flowers, herbs or vegetables from such seed try keeping some of the seed back; not only does this save you having to buy seeds again the following year but it helps maintain the genetic diversity of the world's seeds, which is needed for healthy crops. The edibles most easiest to save are peas, beans, lettuce, peppers and tomatoes.

Other Activities

If you don't have a garden of your own but would like to get involved in growing, look for gardening clubs, local foraging walks and volunteering in your community. Litter-pickers and people to work on recycling are always welcome.

Head Space

Generally in this book I encourage you to move from your head into your heart; however, for this activity you are allowed to use your little grey cells. If you don't have one already, I suggest you get yourself a good field guide appropriate for your area to help you identify plants. Also gather books, websites, apps, magazines and photos of the flora of your area.

Research will expand and enhance your knowledge of the plants that you are meeting and growing. As a rule I always like to cross-reference at least three different herbals or gardening books when researching medicinal herbs or new plants for the garden. With all the information that you are picking up from your sensory observations with the plants, you will also have gained a more holistic view of the plants that you are working with. It's always fascinating and often very reassuring to seek confirmation of what your hunch told you about a plant, but always do your own research too by hanging out with a plant first. Treat yourself to the academic intellectual activity of reading up in books after you have spent time getting to know a plant, otherwise it is much harder to approach it with fresh eyes and with no preconceived notions of how it will appear.

If you are looking up a medicinal plant, you will come across what are referred to as 'herbal actions'; these are a useful way of categorizing medicinal plants depending on what response they cause in the body's physiology. Some common actions are: antiseptic, adaptogen, astringent, diuretic, laxative, stimulant and tonic. Medicinal herbs may also be categorized depending on which organ(s) of the body they affect.

By adding the mental research element to your personal physical and sensory experience of each plant, you will be able to build up a truly holistic and balanced view of plants that you will remember.

I suggest you compile your own materia medica, or collection of plant monographs – these are plant profiles, like a biography, that detail a holistic view of the plant, its physical appearance and properties and your own experience of its personality and characteristics. You may wish to include pressings of the plant's flowers and leaves, detailed drawings and any other creative works that have been inspired by your experience with the plant.

You will also come across fascinating stories and folklore while you are researching plants and this will give you further insight into their uses as well as the personality of the plant and how historically its spirit has interacted with the people in your area. I am continually collecting stories about plants from the people that I meet. One client, for example, recommends always having cactus in the home to ward off burglars. My mother on the other hand always likes to have a mountain ash in the garden to ensure protection (and this was the first plant I planted in the first home that I owned).

Chapter Summary

Getting hands-on with plants in the ways suggested in this chapter is another practical approach to broaden your experience of the plant world. Through this direct interaction, your physical senses will be absorbing and remembering information to deepen your connections and relationship with plants. Ask the plant enthusiasts, herbalists and gardeners you know for their tips and stories and you will gather a rich living library of plant customs that you can adopt.

KEY POINTS

- Experience the life cycle of a plant to really get to know it intimately.
- Find easy-to-grow seeds or pot plants that you have the capacity to look after.
- Experiment by making simple herbal medicines and adding fresh herbs to your diet.
- Research plants and add this to your own personal experience to create a personal materia medica of plant monographs.

Now that you know them with your physical senses, it's time to explore plants as conscious beings and expand your own consciousness to experience the spirit of the plant.

Connect with Plant Consciousness:
Meet the Spirit of Plants

We live in a dynamic, animate and interconnected universe and plants, though seemingly quiet and immobile at first glance compared to we humans' fast-paced lifestyle, are ready to play a much greater role for you. Now that you have explored the natural world around you with your physical senses, your heart and curiosity will most probably be sensing a deeper pathway to explore. If you have skipped most of the exercises from the previous chapters because you are more interested in meeting the spirit of the plants, then I urge you to backtrack slightly. Slow down and spend the time getting to know the plants around you with all of your senses; from this place of knowing you will encounter the song of the universe – it will creep in one day. With time and persistence, nature will succeed in finding her way into your heart, and not just through the physical senses that we have up to now been exploring.

To learn the language of nature you must challenge your ordinary perceptions and change your consciousness. This chapter focuses on the invisible vibration that connects us to our plant friends. You will have already noticed it by now or been touched in some way by the spirit of the plants. I have also included my favourite exercises to guide you to connect to the spirit of plants through meditation, ceremony, prayer, plant essences and shamanic journeying. Experiment, have fun and allow yourself to be guided.

Breathing with the Yew

I sat one afternoon in a circle of ancient yews.
Holding council, on top of a yew throne.
The air was still, abuzz with fairy magic and certainty.
'Who speaks first?' I wanted to know
'It is I,' a voice from the dark corner bellowed

'Say your piece,' I offered
'It is done.'
This is the beauty in the stillness held by the yew.
This is the magic of the shadows cast by the yew.
This is the power of the energy held by the yew.
This is the depth of the wisdom owned by the yew.
Do yew come to us with an open heart?
Do yew come to us for a new start?
Do yew come asking for healing light?
We start in your throat and creep into your heart.
Yew holds power of the ages, ability to splice a man in two,
magic of the Druids and energy rising.
What can I do?
Be still and receive.
Receive.
Open up and receive.
Breathe and receive.

EXERCISE Breathing from the Heart

As discussed in Chapter 4, we are already linked with plants, through our breath. When we focus on this and consciously connect to the plant by giving and receiving breath, we find ourselves intimately connected to the plant and it can be a very moving experience.

After you have spent some time observing and hanging out with a plant that wishes to interact with you and that you wish to get to know better, try the exercise below and meet the plant consciously with your breath. Once you get the hang of it you can choose to consciously breathe in this way whenever you are out in nature. This exercise is inspired by the Green Breath, which was developed by Pam Montgomery and features in her book *Plant Spirit Healing*.

Get yourself comfortable near the plant of your choice and make sure you have appropriately introduced yourself, presented an offering and explained your intention to get to know the plant better and share the breath of life. If at any stage you don't have a good feeling about doing this then try working with a different plant, or try again another day.

Begin by focusing on your breath and grounding into the space that you are in. As thoughts arise, just observe them come and let them go.

If you want to, experiment with circular breathing: breathe in through your nose and out through your mouth. In doing this you may also become aware of the scent of the plant connecting to you.

As you breathe in and out place your attention into your heart.

If you enjoy visualizations, visualize your breath travelling towards the plant as you exhale and visualize breath (or light) travelling from the plant towards you as you inhale. Each time as you inhale and exhale, the breath is travelling into and out of your heart.

I also like to use the following mantra:

'I breathe you' (as I inhale) and 'You breathe me' (as I exhale).

Stay with the breath, the visualization or the mantra for at least 20 minutes.

Notice what occurs in your body and your emotions. You may even feel as though you have begun to merge with the plant.

When you feel ready to leave, tell yourself that you are ending your conscious connection with the plant, give thanks to the plant and leave the area.

Make notes of the thoughts, feelings and sensations that arose as you were doing the exercise.

During our first year running the flower farm, I experienced a gradual opening to nature consciousness and, if you are a gardener or someone who likes to enjoy the outdoors, you will be familiar with this feeling too. It's a feeling, a way of being, that ensures that every time we are outside we find our hearts searching for a green space, for a living, thriving example of the plant world for us to acknowledge.

While nature has this subtle way of permeating our hearts and lodging herself there to grow and blossom, she also enjoys a dramatic element of surprise when she really wants your attention in a big way. Think of the last time you were out for a walk or a drive and turned the corner to see, suddenly, a breathtaking vista that left you speechless and in a state of awe.

I first noticed that the spirit of nature had touched me when I realized I was singing (a lot!) while I was out in the greenhouse and elsewhere. If you, like me are tone deaf you will realize the horror with which I admit this act. I was singing out loud in the fields, singing while planting, singing while harvesting, singing to the trees while walking the dog, singing to the sun as it set … You get the picture! I was singing my heart out to those wonderful plants every day. Each plant had a definite song.

The salvias one year, for example, were full of sadness; it was sorrowful harvesting those flowers – it took for ever and I would often get weepy. Snapdragons on the other hand were always jolly and such a delight. Where did these songs come from? My heart. If you have tried the exercise in Chapter 6 asking a plant for a song then you may feel the same way.

EXERCISE The Beauty of Nature

Stand outside on a non-rainy day, preferably somewhere you can surround yourself with or at least absorb fully a beautiful scene from nature. I am really fortunate and blessed because within moments of stepping outside my front door I am among trees, fields and hillsides. If you are more urban, then head out of your front door with the intention of finding beauty in nature. You may settle in your garden, find yourself in a park or discover a quiet leafy residential street where the sun is shining.

Here in your spot of beauty, absorb the scene with all of your senses.

Open your eyes and fully observe the colours, the way the light reflects, the way the plants interact with the sky, the earth and each other.

Open your ears and start to really listen for the subtle sounds that are going on beyond the more obvious noise.

Open your nose and breathe, open up that sense of smell to whatever might be present.

Open your sense of touch and start to feel the interaction of this scene with your skin. Perhaps there is wind, moisture, cold or warm air surrounding you. Or perhaps there is something luring you that you physically want to touch and grab hold of to know how it would feel against your skin.

Open your mouth and breathe here as if you were swallowing the entire scene with one single gulp. Is there a taste left in your mouth? Is there a sensation left on the tip of your tongue? What words would describe these?

Open your heart and breathe here as if you are breathing in the natural scene in front of you. As if you are breathing all that you see, hear, smell, touch and taste, into your heart. Allow your heart to open more to hold this beauty and life.

Tell the scene in front of you of the beauty that you see, hear, smell, touch and taste.

A simple whisper of 'You are beautiful' is enough, but see what flows. Perhaps you need to express to each living, growing part of nature that you are experiencing how beautiful it really is to you.

Spend as long as you need to in this space of simply honouring, simply recognizing the beauty that is growing and glowing around you.

Pause, be still, breathe for ten breaths and allow a response. Feel for the response in your body.

Now ask whichever of these questions feels right, but adjust the wording as you see fit, to correspond to the scene that you have in front of you:

May I be beautiful like the trees that I see? May I be beautiful like you? May I be colourful like the flowers that I see? May I be graceful with the passing of the seasons? May I be strong and elegant? May I be flowing and purposeful? May I be alive with the spirit of nature? May I be supported and nourished by the earth? May I shine in the light of the sun? May I be beautiful among my peers? May I be determined to grow no matter what? May I be certain of my path?

Keep the questions flowing until you feel you have expressed enough. Again, pause, be still, breathe for ten breaths and allow a response. Feel for the response in your body.

When you are ready to leave your area of beauty say a thank you before heading home. Write down everything in your journal, even the simplest of things – these often carry the most power.

Shamanic Journeying to Connect with the Spirit of a Plant

Shamen around the world have for millennia used the power of sound as a healing tool to enter a state of altered consciousness in order to travel to realms of non-ordinary reality and communicate with the spirit world. The use of instruments like a rattle and the handheld single frame drum allow the shaman to 'ride' the sound waves created by the instrument into another dimension to consult with the spirit world in non-ordinary reality and find information to help a person or community to heal.

The repetitive beat of a drum or rattle slows our brainwaves down to what is known as a theta state, which can help us connect with the spirit of plants and deepen our understanding of their medicine. By medicine, I am referring to the special unique essence that each plant carries that it may be willing to share with you, and which will help your path unfold.

Psychoactive plants such as peyote, ayahuasca, salvia, San Pedro and various types of mushrooms can also be used to experience an altered state of consciousness and connect to the spirit world. To experience the plant spirit medicine of these powerful teachers it's vital for you to be supported and to treat the plants with the respect that they deserve. I would suggest doing so with a qualified shamanic practitioner, who will not only hold the sacred ceremony for you to experience the plant medicine in a safe and protected space but will also be there afterwards to help you integrate the experience in a practical way to benefit your life.

We do not have to be trained shamanic practitioners, though, to work with a drum to experience an altered state of consciousness. A drumming journey can be undertaken at home and with a little practice you can venture into another reality, which may feel like a dream. In this invisible realm you can meet the spirit of a plant you wish to interact with. If you would like to experience a drumming journey, listen to the drumming I have recorded for you here at www.plantsthatspeak.com.

Choose a time when you are not going to be interrupted for at least 30 minutes, turn off your telephone and other distractions and prepare your sacred space.

You may like to place part of your chosen plant or an image of it on your altar to help you feel that the plant is present with you and remind you of your focus. However, a physical representation of the plant is not necessary because you will be meeting the spirit of the plant in your journey, not its physical form. I find it easiest to lie down comfortably, covered with a blanket to keep warm. You may also like to use an eye mask or scarf to cover your eyes. One of the most important elements of any shamanic journey work is intention, so spend a few minutes considering your intention for this journey.

A suggestion for an intention would be 'To Meet the Spirit of (name your chosen plant) and find out more about the plant.' Write down your intention before you begin and hold it in your heart.

Think about a specific question that you may want to ask the plant. This can be as simple as 'Do you like living here?' or more personal, maybe 'Show me your medicine.' It is also wise to offer your assistance to a plant in return for their wisdom and friendship, so hold in your heart the intention to be shown what the plant needs from you.

When you are ready to begin the drumming journey meditation play the link, lie back and listen to it through to the end. You may prefer to experience a drumming journey live in which case enlist a friend to drum for you or if you have your own drum then take yourself on the journey.

As you listen to the drum focus on your breath and your heart centre as if you are breathing the beat of the drum into your heart. Imagine yourself entering into your inner garden and sitting next to your chosen plant. Hold your intention in your mind and open up your senses to really feel that you are in your garden out in nature.

Allow the drum to send you on an adventure with the plant and approach everything that you see and experience with childlike curiosity. Remember your enthusiasm for discovery when you were a child. Feel your heartbeat with each stroke of the drum. Know you have rhythm and open yourself up to the song and dance of the natural world as guided by the drum. Don't make an effort to control your experience; just see where the drum and your mind's eye take you. Allow what comes. You may feel sensations in your body, experience emotion, see colours – the possibilities are endless. You may experience the journey as you do a dream. Try not to analyze your experience as you are experiencing it; simply observe and feel into it with the intention of remembering.

When you hear the rhythm of the drum change, this is an indication that the journey will soon be drawing to a close. So take this time to give thanks for whatever has appeared during your journey. You will begin to hear the drum change again (it will rapidly speed up); this is your call to return to everyday life. Before you do so, give thanks for your experience, whatever that was. Then, leave your garden, shut the gate and walk up the stairs. Return yourself to the room.

When the drumming finishes, stretch and wake your body up gradually. Drink a glass of water and stamp your feet to ground yourself.

Take out your journal and note everything you can remember from your journey.

Since shamanic drumming journeys can be very similar to dreams you may find it useful to note your experience by themes, key elements or with colour in a drawing rather than in a linear format. For more ideas of how to do this check out the section on dreams in the next chapter.

There is no right or wrong way to experience a journey, so try not to be disappointed if you fall asleep or didn't experience anything. Remember this is a technique that takes practice and you can come back to this journey again and again. In my personal practice my preferences for journeying have evolved over time. My initial experiences were mainly listening to a drumming track while lying down, but over time as my involvement in drumming circles has become more frequent, I have found that an embodied journey – with movement and dance to the sound of a live drum or rattle, either my own or other people's sound – gives me much more insight and makes it easier for me to connect. I also find that the use of a drum or a rattle outside in nature is a wonderful way to connect with the earth. If you find that you are interested in exploring more about shamanism and how to connect to the spirit of all things in this way, then I suggest you take a course with an experienced shamanic practitioner or find a workshop that you can participate in.

If you would prefer to connect with the invisible aspect of a plant through meditation and visualization then refer back to the Meditation 'to Experience Yourself as a Garden' from Chapter 2. This time, when you are in your garden, imagine a plant that you have just met growing inside your inner garden. Sit by it, watch it grow and breathe together. Notice where it grows in your inner garden, how it grows and what stage of growth it is at. Spend as much time with your plant in your garden as you need.

One of the first plants that I started consciously working with was willow. Having planted many of the young plants on our property, and feeling familiar with the plant from my childhood, it seemed pretty natural for me to spend time with willow. On this particular spring day I spent the entire morning observing a lovely large willow by the lake. I introduced myself and started my observations, getting to know the plant. I held in my heart the intention to meet it and receive healing. I offered the willow a pinch of the home-grown tobacco that I make it my habit to always carry. I got out my journal and made striking marks of blue and yellow (not really the colours you might associate with willow!).

My initial impression was one of awe and overwhelm – there seemed to be so much energy whizzing around this plant; I was astounded. I felt that the plant was really showing me how to grow. Willow has an incredible capacity to grow; you can simply cut a branch and plant it in the ground and it will take root. I also used to use a strong infusion of willow as a rooting hormone when taking hardwood cuttings in the greenhouse to help encourage their growth and increase their chances of taking root and growing well.

So I spent some time mark-making and absorbing the vibrant energy of the willow. After touching the plant I then started to consciously breathe with it, breathing in and out through my heart, receiving and giving breath and light from and to this marvellous specimen. It was joyful. After a while a song came to me and I started swaying around and singing the willow song to myself. My voice then became loud, no longer secret and hidden within me. The song of the willow took hold of me, pulling up hidden emotions deep inside. As a result I started sobbing, heartfelt, deep-rooted tears of loss and sadness, of nostalgia, of love and opportunity long gone.

It was a moving, strongly emotional experience and a powerful healing. It seemed an age but the flow did come to an end and after I had danced the willow dance, sung the willow song and cried my willow tears, I thanked the plant and retreated inside.

Later in the day I journeyed with my drum to discover more of willow. Willow breaks through boundaries and brings growth and vibrancy. My journey with willow took me through the roots of a tree I knew in my childhood and showed me a hive of activity. I had a sense of many helpers there to support me. After my drumming journey I felt full of hope and wonder and excited by life again.

I continue to feel full of gratitude and admiration for the willow and I know who to call on when I need a burst of vibrant energy to shift me into a new state of being and leave behind old stagnation.

Grounding and Integration

When we are working with invisible realms we can have a tendency to drift 'off with the fairies' into these other worlds. While this is a lovely state to be in and perfect for communicating with the plant spirits and other elementals, in order to function in the human reality of this earthly plane, drive cars, answer emails and so forth, we do need to be grounded in this reality.

A simple grounding exercise is to walk barefoot outside on the grass or touch your hands to the earth and imagine there are roots that grow from your hands or feet to reach right down into the earth. This brings you right back into your body and back down to earth. Likewise, drinking a warm cup of tea, eating a handful of nuts or taking five deep breaths right down into your belly are other good exercises to fully ground you in the here and now. Make it a regular habit to always ground yourself after working with plant consciousness or other energies.

Allowing ample time to be still in order to integrate the experience into your whole being is also vital to complete the process and benefit from the shifts that can take place.

If you end your drumming journey or meditation and step immediately back into 'real life' without pausing to let the experience settle, you could miss valuable insight.

I think of it like a snow globe that has been shaken and needs time to settle again. As the snow globe settles the landscape comes back into view and may look slightly different. Resist the temptation to rush back into your day. Rest, settle, integrate, observe, open to receive this new shift and ground yourself before you step back into the world again.

In my personal practice, I find that it is during the stillness of this integration period that insight and clarity appear for me. I often listen to a piece of gentle music while my experience settles. This period of integration feels as valuable as the meditation or journey that I have experienced, so make sure to allow ample time for this part of your practice.

Flower Essences

In simple terms, a flower essence is an infusion or decoction of flowers in spring water that has a powerful effect on the emotions and mental well-being. The way that they work is through the energetic imprint of the life force or essence of the plant interacting with the essence of our energy and our spirit. I recommend using flower essences as another way of empowering your interaction with the energies of the plants that grow around you. They can feel very supportive as you can literally carry the essence of the plant with you about your person and consume it when necessary.

There are many flower essences available out there to discover, but it is even more exciting and empowering to have a go at creating your own! Flower essences are excellent tools to aid emotional healing, especially when we are stuck in a certain pattern. They have a way of gently unravelling tight, hard or stagnant energy and getting us back to centre and into harmony with our feelings and being. I like that they are a simple, gentle and practical way of experiencing plant spirit medicine. The essences are easy to administer (you just take a few drops in water) and also a great way to get in touch with your feelings and become more aware of yourself and your role here on earth.

One sleepy Sunday about five years ago I decided that today was the day to make my first ever flower essence. I had been giving it a lot of thought for quite some time and despite the long list of Sunday chores to get done, I couldn't resist the opportunity on this bright sunny day when I saw the bright yellow blooms of dandelion across the field. Selecting and harvesting the flowers and placing them in spring water was joyous and beautiful. I sat next to the bowl of spring water and flowers watching them infuse under the bright sun and I felt full of cheer. I was wrapped in a warm, fuzzy, loving and sensuous bubble of peace and beauty. I physically felt my shoulders drop about an inch and my whole body relax. I stayed in that bubble all day. I took out a journal, laid myself down on a bench in the sun and let myself relax, as if I was on holiday and had nothing better to do than lounge by the pool. For the entire day, while I strained and bottled the dandelion essence, I continued to experience its relaxing properties.

The message I received that day was 'Relax and enjoy life,' and it was just what I needed! I am eternally grateful to dandelion for this medicine and now I have it bottled as an essence and always on hand, even during the winter when the bright dandelion flowers are not blooming. I use the wonderful essence by taking just a few drops in water. It opens my heart to look on the bright side of life and reminds me to relax and find the joy. It is brilliant for people, like me, who cram so much into their days that they end up exhausted and unable to achieve everything and end up feeling a bit stressed and dissatisfied on top of all that fatigue. Whenever I take the dandelion essence, I always feel like putting my feet up, having a cup of tea and reading a good book, despite the huge to-do list that is usually waiting for me!

Pointers for Making Flower Essences

Only make essences from flowers that you feel are really talking to you.

Read through the steps and then follow your intuition as guidance; don't worry about doing the process 'correctly' but relax and follow the flow. You will be guided by the plants themselves.

Make sure you have a bright sunny day ahead of you and when the sun rises, select your plant and sit for 15 minutes breathing with it. Make your intention clear, i.e., 'I would like to gather your flowers to create a liquid essence that carries your vibration and medicine to help those who use it.'

When you feel ready, start gathering the flowers. I don't like to touch them directly with my hands (it would infuse my energy with them) so I always use tongs to hold the flowers.

Gather your flowers and place them into a glass bowl of spring water beside the plant.

At this point I always choose to sit in meditation, breathing with the plant again. I then usually end up taking out my drum or rattle and make sounds and sing by the side of the plant.

Make sure you always offer a token of your thanks and leave the plant and the flowers in the bowl for the day.

Before the sun goes down return to the plant and the bowl of flowers. Strain the liquid into a jar – this is your mother essence. You may feel guided to leave the flowers that are left after this process somewhere significant. Pause by the plant, notice if the process feels complete and ask for guidance if something feels like it needs to happen. If you have not already, ask the plant to show you how the essence can be used and who can benefit from it. Even though I have some great books on flower essences, I never look up their meanings until I after I have worked with them, so that my mind and heart remain open and not fixed on an idea.

Use the essence immediately or, to make it last, add alcohol like brandy or vodka as a preservative. You can take a few drops of the essence in water, bathe in it, make a spray… the list is endless.

You will find your experience with plant essences fascinating and blissful. It is a wonderful way to connect with flowers and will give you a new appreciation for them.

Plant Ceremony

There has recently been and continues to be an increase in popularity of trips to the Amazon for westerners to attend ayahuasca ceremonies with the curanderos of the area. The celebrity of these teacher plants, great and powerful though they are, has rather overshadowed our native British plants. Many students of plant medicine are seeking ceremonies far afield rather than opening their eyes and hearts to honouring the plant life that grows beside them at home.

I love ceremony of all shapes and sizes and so do plants. Ceremony helps us shift our perspective from our ordinary reality into another space and opens up doorways to the invisible realms. You might feel that the idea of ceremony is associated with religion and so wish to reject the idea altogether, but I would encourage you to feel into the idea creatively and with an open mind to find something that will be in your comfort zone.

Plant ceremonies are an opportunity to honour the plants, seek guidance, expand our consciousness to meet their plant spirit, be shown their wisdom or ask for help. Involving nature consciousness in our ceremonies is as easy as burying a written paper list of old habits that we want to release in the earth and asking the earth for her help. You can combine plant ceremony with celebrations and also include plant diets, as discussed in Chapter 6.

Five Lessons I Learned from an Ecuadorian Shaman

Twenty or so years ago, I was a student in Ecuador. I would love to say that I was on a spiritual mission, but at that stage of my life, it was a different variety of connection with spirits that fuelled my lifestyle. However, as you will also have experienced, life always has a way of providing us with the experiences that we need. As it so happens, as I was chatting to my friend Jose Luis one day he revealed that his plans for the following evening were to attend a ceremony with his shaman, Pepe. It was such a casual mention, just as you would talk about a yoga class or a dentist appointment – no big deal. I was intrigued and I asked if I could come too. My request befuddled my friend; there had never been any westerners present at the ceremonies, so he had no idea whether or not it was actually allowed. As luck would have it, I was able to attend and it really was one of the most incredible events of my life. I won't detail the ceremony here, not because it is secret but because it really was sacred and magical.

If you are ever to experience your own shamanic ceremony with plant medicine, having read about my experience won't add to yours; in fact it is more likely to take away something of the intensity and the magic. So instead I would like to share five key learnings that have shaped my life and which I still go by today.

1. **There is spirit in everything. Everything is sacred.**
   This became strongly apparent to me when we entered the ceremonial space. Everything in the room and on the mesa (centrepiece) was vibrating as if it was alive. The sacred space and focus of the ceremony really amplified this aspect and ever since then I have tried to bring the sacred into the everyday, to continue to honour the spirit in everything. Rocks, trees, rivers, the weather, plants, places, people… everything!

2. **Honour Mother Earth and all her gifts.**
   During the ceremony I felt such a deep connection to Mother
   Earth as the creator and mother of all things. Everything
   included in the ceremony was blessed and dedicated to Mother
   Earth or *Pacha Mama*. This made such a big impact on me;
   I had never before thanked the sun for shining, I had never
   thanked the earth for supporting and nourishing me. So the
   message from this is linked to the first lesson – yes there is spirit
   in everything and yes we must honour it and bless it. This gives it
   power and meaning and a deeper purpose for our lives.

3. **There is power in ceremony and ritual.**
   Gathered together as we were with focus and intent, in a space that
   had been blessed and prepared in a meaningful way, the strength
   and power pulsing through the people in the space, connecting us
   all, was deep and powerful. I realized I had no ceremony or ritual
   or anything sacred in my life – and that in not including these
   things in my life, I was missing out on a huge amount of power
   and opportunity for connection and transformation. I asked myself
   'When am I going to start making things sacred?' If you make things
   sacred then you can benefit from the momentum, vitality and spirit
   in the actions that you take.

4. **There is more than one reality!**
   Is this reality that we live in, that we think is real, really real?
   The ceremony was a shape-shifting, mind-bending experience
   that left me questioning, what was real. It was exhilarating,
   blissful, ecstatic – but at the same time, I was in a small dark
   room in the backstreets of the city of Quito. How was this even
   possible? All this left me questioning what is reality and what
   can I create; asking, can I change my reality?

5. **We are all connected; create community.**
   Within the vibrant, animated, magical buzz created by the sacred
   space and intention of the ceremony and the people present,
   I felt truly connected to the cosmic web of life and supported by
   a much greater force. It's this sense of connection that not only
   opened my heart compassionately to all beings but helped me to

feel the strength and power of this unity. It made me long for and see the enormous value in community.

I remember walking out of the ceremony at the end. I had no idea of the time, as we had been in the ceremony all night. I stepped out into the early hours of the morning as the sun was rising and I felt that my eyes were open for the first time in a long time. The colours looked so vivid. Everything looked so alive.

After the ceremony something in me did change for ever, although not in the way that you might imagine. Experiences like this don't necessarily send us off like skyrockets on our mission; they often lead us down yet another path, along which we meander, may even go off track, take steps backwards and so forth. One ceremony does not heal everything – but these lessons are still with me today.

Ceremony Begins at Home

If you have a garden then I suggest holding a ceremony at meaningful moments throughout the year to honour the plants and wildlife that grow and to feel into what the garden needs.

Each year on the farm we would hold a ceremony in the spring to bring in the new, asking for growth and abundance. We used it as an opportunity to remind the land what we needed from it and to tune ourselves in to perceiving what it in turn might need from us. Around a large fire, we would give many offerings and much song. At the end of the growing season, as the first frost killed the flowers and put an end to our market sales for the year, we would hold another ceremony. This was more focused on giving thanks for the harvest and then turning our thoughts inward as we followed the seasons into winter.

By carrying out ceremonies like this on the land, we gain a deeper connection to places and a deeper understanding of nature consciousness. It can be as simple as deciding to have a fire in the autumn or spring to tidy away all the physical matter that is no longer needed; but with the right intention, this simple action can also help you burn away any emotional and mental clutter that is no longer serving you.

Simple rituals like giving prayers and blessings when watering plants also connect you to the spirit of the plant and can be a powerful practice. Try mindfully watering a plant and saying a prayer, like 'May you be healthy' or 'May you grow strong.'

Limpias and Plant Prayers

By singing to your seeds as you plant them and whispering sweet words of blessing and intention over your herbal concoctions as you chop, infuse and blend, you can really potentize your home-grown plants and remedies.

I like to harvest herbs and tell them of the journey I wish to take them on. Asking the nettle, for example, for its young tops to take home and make a soup for friends who are joining us for dinner that night. Or singing to the St John's wort as I harvest its flower buds and petals to make an infused oil to be made into a salve for burns and bruises.

Saying prayers and blessings is particularly beneficial whenever you are making a medicine or harvesting flowers with a specific person in mind, as you can tell the plant the story of the person and their suffering and ask for the plant's specific medicine to give them the healing that they require.

A limpia is a traditional cleansing carried out by a healer in which a bundle of herbs and flowers is brushed over a client's body while various chants and prayers are uttered. Imagine being brushed by flowers from head to foot. Bliss!

A simple example of a prayer or mantra to repeat while doing this is: 'I give thanks to the spirit of the plant and have faith with all of my heart that (plant name) will help me/my client for the highest good of all beings.'

BLESSING How to Give a Plant Blessing to a Friend

- Take a deep breath in, into your heart, down into your belly, then allow yourself to relax as you breathe out.
- Call on a higher power: your personal guides, angels, ancestors, spirit helpers etc.
- Silently ask for help with **one** simple thing – this can be something your friend is working on healing physically or emotionally or a challenge they are facing. Ask for guidance, strength, love or blessings that are for your friend's highest good and the good of all beings, NOT material things.
- Ask the person receiving to stretch their hands out in front of them.
- Place plants on the pulse points of each wrist, top of the head, heart and womb (for men go to the area just below the belly button).

- If you feel directed to, you may place plants over the chakras, the energy centres that run down the body from the crown to the root chakra. Use your intuition and go where you feel guided. I also like to include the feet.
- Keep breathing into your heart, and as you breathe out bring your breath from your heart into your belly.
- Keep the circle of belly–heart breathing going.
- When you feel ready, finish the prayer and give thanks.
- Do not use those flowers or plants again for a blessing; dispose of them respectfully.

In my one-to-one treatments I commonly use simple plant prayers to ask for guidance and healing. By doing this I am simply asking for the essence or spirit of the plant to be present for a client and to offer their medicine.

Marigold has such bright flowers and a very strong scent; it is said that it is the only flower that spirits on the other side can smell. I have often found it to be a keen participant in ceremony and blessings, as this next story illustrates.

One evening I was rushing to gather my drum and other personal items to take with me to a drumming circle. Marigold had been on my mind lately because we grew giant African marigolds and they were particularly tall and radiant at this time of year, and the bright flowers had such a strong fragrance that they could not be ignored. I had every intention of bringing some of the flowers to the circle to share with the women present. However, when I arrived and we began smudging to open the circle, I realized that I had left those lovely flowers behind.

My friend holding the circle turned to me and said: 'Fay, I get the sense there is something that you meant to bring with you that wants to be here.'

I could only agree and explained about the marigolds. I was then sent off to her garden to pick some of her marigolds, and only after I had returned with a handful could the circle begin. The marigolds had clearly decided that they needed to be part of the evening's activities.

I proceeded to introduce everyone in the circle to the flowers and then performed a short limpia with them for everyone.

Everyone was filled with the sunshine, peace and sense of joy that these flowers bring. Marigold had done her job and was clearly pretty pleased! What a blessing for us all. Thank you marigold.

Guideline for a Simple
Honouring Ceremony

Don't get bound up in rules and instructions when engaging in ceremony; what is important is that you create something that has personal meaning for you. In this way the ceremony will strengthen your connection with both your inner spirit and the plants that you are inviting in.

Choose and prepare the area for your ceremony. Cleanse the space appropriately (see the discussion on smudging in Chapter 2).

Gather a group of friends and invite them to a ceremony to honour their favourite plant. Each person needs to come to the ceremony with their chosen plant. To prepare for the ceremony, you may want to prepare by fasting, or preparing a special infusion of your own chosen plant, or by simply harvesting the plants with the intention to use them in the ceremony. You may wish to have a special set of clothes, or an accessory like a sash, hat, mask or special jewellery, set aside to wear for the ceremony. This is a way of helping you to step out of your ordinary life and into a new reality.

On the day of the ceremony, gather your friends in a circle and open the space in a way that feels right for you. Over time you will find words and ways with which you feel comfortable. I usually welcome the directions using my drum and rattle to call to my ancestors and helping spirits in a way similar to the following, which is influenced by my shamanic and Druidic training:

'I call on my ancestors, spirit guides, angels and the spirit of this place. I honour you and give thanks for your presence here in our ceremony and for holding your divine light in this space to keep us safe and protected for our gathering here today.'

(Turning to face the east) 'I give thanks to the spirit of the east. Thank you for new beginnings, the element of air and the winged and feathered ones. I honour you and all the plant beings of the east, of Asia.'

(Turning to face the south) 'I give thanks to the spirit of the south. Thank you for the creative fire and passion in my soul, and the sun. I honour you and all the plant beings of the hot south, of Africa, of the desert plains.'

(Turning to face the west) 'I give thanks to the spirit of the west. Thank you for showing me the power of emotion, the element of water, the bear and leaping salmon. I honour you and all the plant beings of the west, of the rainforests of the Amazon.'

(Turning to face the north) 'I give thanks to the spirit of the north and the place of my ancestors. Thank you for being my guiding star. I honour you and all the plant beings of the great expanse of the north, the plants that survive in the coldest of temperatures.'

(Bending to touch the earth) 'I give thanks to Mother Earth. Thank you for your constant support and nourishment in every action that I take. I honour you, all that you give me and every being that grows from your fertile land.'

(Standing with arms outstretched) 'I give thanks to Father Sky, the moon and stars. Thank you for the light that you shine down upon me to help me and all the other plant beings grow. I honour you.'

(Standing with hands on heart) 'I give thanks to the spirit that rests within me. I know that I am not my body. I know that I am not alone, I am connected in the web of life to all things. I honour this connection to the spirit that lives within all things.'

Then ask everyone to sit down in a circle. If you are leading the ceremony begin by stating its intention, which in this case is to honour your special plant friends at this time.

To get a sense of the energy present in the circle you may want to pass around a talking stick, feather or stone to give each person an opportunity to introduce themselves and say a few words about what brought them to the ceremony and how they are feeling.

After this, sing a song and play your drums to get some energy flowing in the circle.

When you feel the time is right go round the circle and allow each person the opportunity to introduce the group to their plant. Let them speak about three things that they love about the plant, why they chose it and how it makes them feel. If they have made an infusion then pass that round the group for everyone to taste; if they have the plant or part of the plant with them then pass this round the group too so that each person gets the opportunity to spend some time with the plant. Honour the plant in a way that seems appropriate. You may wish to dance, drum or sing, or speak words that the plant evokes.

Keep going round the circle of people and meeting each plant until everyone has introduced their plants to the group.

When this is complete the person holding the circle can lead a drumming journey so that each member of the circle can journey to meet the spirit of a plant of their choice (it does not have to be the plant that they came with). Or everyone in the circle can sing and drum together and invite the plant spirits in. Suggest everyone journeys with an intention of asking the plant about its medicine.

Lead the drumming journey and afterwards, go round the circle giving everyone an opportunity to share their experience.

Feel into what else is needed – perhaps more singing, drumming or dancing. Perhaps someone in the ceremony requires specific healing and a plant prayer or blessing would be appropriate.

When it is time for your ceremony to come to an end, close the space appropriately by giving thanks to the ancestors, helping spirits and directions that you welcomed in at the beginning and that have been present throughout the ceremony. Extinguish any candles and make it clear that this space is closed and the work is complete.

Complete your ceremony with a feast of good food and wine!

Ceremony is Celebration

If the idea of ceremony is unusual for you then it might help you to think of it more as a focused celebration. The idea is simply to celebrate and honour plants, nature or Mother Earth in whatever way feels right for you. You may like to create a small ritual of giving plants in your garden a blessing of something like wine or honey, to show your gratitude for their energy and beauty. You could draw the word 'Love' or a big heart in the soil to show your gratitude to your garden or favourite place in nature.

Celebrating in this way can be short and sweet or long and elaborate – whatever you choose; as always it is the intention that counts. The most important thing, as it is a celebration, is to make it joyful and fun!

Questions for Self-reflection

1. After trying some of these exercises to meet the spirit of a plant, have you discovered anything new? Has anything surprised you?
2. You have acquired notes on the physical characteristics of the plants you have met, but now that you have encountered the spirit of the plant, can you give your plant a character profile? What are the special qualities, colours or feelings that the spirit of this plant inspires in you?
3. How do you consider your relationship with this plant?
4. How would you like to use or further experience the plant that you have been working with? Has your plant asked for anything

or given you specific actions to undertake? What about painting a picture, composing a poem, taking a herbal bath with the plant or even wearing it about your person? Be creative!

By exploring the invisible aspect of plants, sensing their special essence and opening up to their consciousness, we are able to experience their unique and special potency. Plants become like a kind of living medicine that acts on mind, body and spirit and can be used in many ways without limiting us to having to physically be in the presence of a plant or physically able to access a part of it.

Chapter Summary

You may have already felt the presence of plant consciousness while you were carrying out the exercises in the previous chapter on using your physical senses; and I hope that the suggestions in this chapter have given you insight into the depth and fun that you can experience while interacting with and getting to know the spirit of a plant.

KEY POINTS

- Breathe together.
- Experience a drumming journey.
- Create space in your meditation.
- Make a flower essence.
- Celebrate in ceremony.
- Explore a way that works for you that you are guided to create!

In the next chapter you will learn about other ways in which the spirit of plants is communicating with you and how to interpret this; and how to consider starting conversations with your favourite plants.

9

Receiving Healing Gifts: Tools for Communication and Interpretation

My whole body is alive with you
My whole body is alive
With your light that radiates through me
With your sound that vibrates into my core
With your gentle touch that sweeps my body to the ground with
adoration, respect and love
My whole body is alive with you
My whole body breathes with you
My whole body lives for you
In my heart I am alive
There is no end to me
to where you begin
as I breathe, the breath I give to you comes back to me,
to complete me
So that I may breathe again
my body is held in your embrace
my body is supported on your land
my whole body is alive
singing with thanks and joy for this day.

— September 2016

I hope that by now, having completed many of the exercises, you have begun to get to know plants more intimately and broaden your view of these magnificent green beings and experience a taste of the wisdom that they hold. Whether you feel more drawn to the physical senses like observation and touch or you prefer the meditative space of the drum journey or breathing with a plant, you will have already picked up a wide variety of plant communications. These, as you may have discovered, can be very subtle, like simple nuances of movement, temperature change and other sensations that you may pick up in your body. Your self-awareness practice will be helping you to maintain your level of awareness and be open and alert to plant responses.

If after spending some time with a plant you don't sense that the plant is being very responsive, never belittle your interaction, just graciously accept the experience and keep experimenting with other plants and with other techniques. If your mind is questioning you, it can be really tempting to brush off your hunches or feelings as 'just your imagination'. Keep in your heart the possibility that everything you are picking up is genuine communication from plants. Make a real effort to stop thinking and instead drop into your body to experience what your body knows about your experiences. This chapter is dedicated to helping you decipher and engage in plant communication and be alert for guidance, healing and messages from all angles, at any time.

Nature's Signposts

In shamanic cultures, it is believed that everything in life has spirit and meaning, like a theatre full of omens and signs that provide us with guidance. These omens are nature's signposts and can lead you to make healthy and wise decisions to grow and shape your beautiful life. As you go about your day, pay attention to the world around you and hold questions in your mind about the life decisions you are facing. If you are walking outside, see what animals and birds you notice, or perhaps the clouds are making certain shapes? Pay attention also to people and conversations that you have directly, as well as snippets you may overhear; these words may contain answers and inspiration for you. So too could songs that you happen to hear on the radio while you are pondering a certain idea. Even adverts on billboards, TV or taxis may be sending you a message that you need to see at this time.

Have you ever experienced a book falling open at a certain page that seems to fit with just what you were needing or thinking about? Or overheard a conversation and thought 'Oh, that's exactly what I was considering!'?

Of course we often call these occurrences coincidences – but Albert Einstein said that coincidence is God's way of remaining anonymous.

The following story about my fern illustrates just how persistent plants can be if they really want to grab our attention.

One spring day I was pottering about my garden, with no particular intention beyond just tidying up and reflecting on the changes that I might want to make in the garden for the coming year.

There was a large fern that had really taken off and was starting to encroach on the small area where we grow our vegetables, I didn't really register it too much other than a fleeting thought of 'Perhaps we need to move that fern.' Later that morning I started leafing through a magazine – not a gardening one or the sort of thing in which that you would expect to find any information about plants, just a regular women's magazine. As I was flicking through the pages I came across a long article about ferns, which included some stories illustrating the magic and folklore associated with them. I was intrigued and lapped up the stories. I'd thought about ferns twice in one day – was this plant trying to tell me something?

I didn't stop to find out at that stage as I had to go out, but that evening I visited a friend's house for the first time and, on entering her living room, I exclaimed in wonder as I met the gigantic fern that she keeps there. She proceeded to tell me another story about the magic of ferns, from her birth country, Poland. I was intrigued – and highly alert now. Three times in one day fern had been trying to get my attention! Now I was really listening.

The fern story that my friend told me was about the rare, magical wild fern flower that only blooms twice a year, on the winter and summer solstice. Great wisdom, wealth and power are bestowed on the person who finds the rare flower, which is hidden in a secluded part of the forest and guarded by many mythological creatures. Like every fairy story, there is a sting in the tale: the great riches from the fern may be taken but can never be shared.

In this version of the story, the young man who has been so desperately seeking his fortune finally gets it – but is then unable to share it with anyone and becomes a lonely miser. What a sad story! It was time for me to sit and reflect on what fern was trying to show me. Where in my life was I not sharing fully? Or where was I not appreciating my current situation and community and instead seeking a fortune that would not lead to happiness?

As you attune to the natural world around you, reaching out with your heart, you will find more meaning reflected back to you from your environment.

Opening to Receive

The amount of information that bombards our sensory receptors on a daily basis is overwhelming, so in order to survive we selectively filter this data to shut out much of the stimulation. As a result I believe that most of us have also dulled our ability to connect to the subtle energies that surround us. A daily meditation practice that encourages stillness and quiet contemplation can play a key role in helping us receive the connection that we are craving.

The exercises in Chapter 6 will have helped you open up the receiving channels in your physical senses to the language of nature. The addition of ceremony, prayer or shamanic journeying in Chapter 7 will have helped you expand your reality and explore the landscape of your imagination and spirit.

If you are struggling, centre yourself for a moment and consider how open you are to receiving. How can you strengthen your ability to receive? What might be stopping you from fully receiving? At the end of your day take stock of all of the physical and invisible information that you have received in that day. Notice which of that information made you feel alive and what drained you? What have you been in contact with that truly resonated deep within you?

Plants, people, objects, places, emotions, events all carry a different vibration and resonance. As you become more used to being in the company of certain plants, and attuning to their vibration, it becomes easier to tune in to different plants of the same family, even if you have never met them before. An example of this might be when you visit a garden and see some plants that, though you have never seen them before, you have a feeling about what they are. This is you recognizing not only their appearance but also the subtle feelings that you pick up in your energy body. Developing this ability and refining our 'dials' to tune in is another tool to help you get to know plants and for me, it certainly is one of the most exciting.

EXERCISE **Receiving the Vibration of a Place**

This exercise will help you to practise receiving the vibration and energy of different places. Start in a place you know well, such as your living room. Close your eyes and allow yourself to settle with five deep breaths. Allow your sense of hearing to absorb the external noises and check in with your body to acknowledge any feelings that you are holding.

When you feel ready, with your eyes still closed drop your awareness down into your heart space and from that place imagine you are sending out little feelers, which are sensing information and at the same time opening up your energy field to receive information. How do you know that you are sitting in your living room? Where do you feel that knowing? What information, excluding the familiar cues of the smell, the sound, the temperature, the sensation of your body on the seat, are you receiving that tells you that this is your living room?

Note down anything that you notice about the feel of this place. Then go outside to a space in nature that you know well and repeat the exercise. As before, with your eyes closed how do you know where you are? In what way does this place feel different from your living room? What subtle and invisible information are you receiving from this place? Keep practising wherever you go to build up these special senses. Repeat the exercise with different trees or plants, just to get a feel for the differences in frequency and resonance that occur.

Dream Time

Another way that plants may interact with you is during your nightly dreams. Most people dream for 100 minutes each night, despite many of us not remembering our dreams at all. Dreams are entertaining nightly adventures, sometimes frightening and often unusual, perhaps nonsensical; often stories that contain a wealth of symbols, if only we could fathom what they mean. Robert Moss is one of my favourite authors on dreams; see the bibliography for more information on his work.

The term lucid dreaming describes the act of becoming aware, during a dream, that you are dreaming and then being able to continue to experience your dream but with full waking consciousness. This means you are able to control your actions within the dream and create the dreamscape. This can be fun and enlightening as you communicate directly with your subconscious.

The first step towards working with dreams is getting into the habit of remembering your dreams on waking and recording them as quickly as you can. To do this, keep a notebook and pen or pencil by your bedside and have it ready and waiting for you when you wake up. If you don't write your dreams down it's likely that they will fade from your memory like disappearing ink.

If you have difficulty remembering your dreams, before you go to bed, focus on the intention to remember them. As you're falling asleep ask for clear dreams that you will be able to remember. You can make a request to a particular plant if you are hoping for its appearance, and, in general, pay particular attention to any appearances in your dreams from the green kingdom.

Keep an image of your notebook in your mind and have the intention of waking up, picking up the notebook and writing down your dreams. This will act as a trigger for your unconscious brain to relate to and remind you to focus on your dreams. It also plants an unconscious intention: to associate the notebook with remembering dreams.

Suggestions on Dream Journaling

- Give the dream a title and date – this will help you recall it later (e.g., call it 'The yellow bus').
- Note the theme of the dream, e.g., Hiding, chasing, searching. This will help you keep track of recurring themes.
- Describe the main event.
- Note the feelings that you experienced during the dream.
- If words are not vibrant enough, try drawing the dream with images, pattern, texture and colour.

Reflection and Interpretation

Before you rush off to purchase a dream dictionary or type your dream or omen into Google in search of its meaning, take a deep breath, pause and turn inwards. The only person who can accurately help you analyze the meaning of your dreams or your journeys is you. Learn to connect to your place of knowing and trust your own sense of interpretation and meaning. Each specific element of a dream communicates something of value, but do not try to fit the elements of your dream into a generic meaning; different things mean different things to different people. For you a bicycle might signify your childhood memories of riding around the yard; for another person it might represent something more sinister, for example if their sister was once injured in a bicycle accident.

Consider each key element in the dream separately and ask yourself: what does that mean to me? What could that represent? Why is that object there like that? Who put it there?

Questions to Ask Yourself

- Where does the dream take place? Is it in one location or does it shift?
- What was the main feeling to the dream? And how do you feel about it now?
- Are you observing the action or are you participating/involved in the dream?
- What/who is the focus or centre of attention in the dream?
- If people appear, how do you feel about them? What might they represent? Has this person appeared before in a similar context?
- Is the dream in colour or black and white? Vibrant or muted?
- How could this dream relate to something that is happening for real in your life, either literally or symbolically?
- Does the dream or the theme of it recur?
- What do the symbols in the dream mean to you? How do they appear?

Many of us are very receptive to guidance that can appear in the form of symbols and metaphors in our dreams when we are in the state of just falling asleep or just about to wake up. I find that these are the moments when I receive key messages from my spirit helpers and plants that have something to say.

A few years ago I was woken up just before my morning alarm by several trees featuring very clearly in my inner vision, and was very surprised when a beautiful coconut palm started talking to me in French. The message I was given was 'Elle a une douleur au coeur' and I kept seeing the sea; I had the impression that this person was overseas or far away from something. I was told that the solution that would help her was 'coco, coco, coco.'

The only person who I could think of that this might be relevant to was a woman who I had met online a few months earlier as part of a Facebook group. Despite this message not making sense to me I had a feeling it would make sense to her, so with some hesitation I sent her a message explaining the information from the coconut palm. Her response was incredible. The message made sense because her ex-partner, the father of her son, lives on an island where coconuts grow and she was in a heart-wrenching situation: full of joy on the one hand as she was about to marry her new partner but torn apart because she hadn't yet told the ex about this decision. She knew that he would be hurt by the news, as they still had strong feelings for each other but circumstance had driven them apart. She was so excited by the message and agreed to take care of herself by finding some coconut water or coconuts and connecting to the energy of the coconut palm for support and strength.

Plant Conversations

One of the questions often on the tip of the tongues of participants of my workshops is: 'Is the plant going to talk to me and how?' Meaning, 'Will I receive a string of words in a language that I understand? Will this be like an external voice having a conversation with me? Will this be words that seem to come through me as if I was speaking or writing? Will this be like an automatic download? Will this be more like feelings and sensations?'

And the answer, as you have probably guessed, is all of the above, plus lots of ways I have forgotten to mention. Plants appear to us and communicate in the ways that we are susceptible or more open to.

I often get asked whether I see plant devas (deva is a Sanskrit word meaning 'shining one'). Many people start trying to communicate with the invisible realms because they are imagining and hoping for visions of plant devas, beautiful characters stepping out of the plant. The more I interact with plants and nature consciousness, the more I experience the plant kingdom as light in different colours, vibration, a strong sense of presence, emotions in my body and degrees of brightness, but I rarely physically see faces or see plants as people when I am outside in nature. Instead I most often catch glimpses of figures out of the corner of my eye.

However, when I am working in the spirit realm, during a shamanic journey for example, plants will often appear to me as people. In this way they are choosing to appear to me as a character that is a meaningful way for me to work with them, maybe as a beautiful woman or as an old man depending on the issue. These are some archetypes that my consciousness is comfortable working with as guides and advisors; for you it may be completely different.

During my five years of flower farming I would often get woken up in the middle of the night by a plant that needed attention. One of the first plants to do this was raspberry. I woke up one night with the distinct knowing that there was someone in the room. Luckily I was very sleepy, so rather than let this freak me out I just relaxed and opened up to its presence; after all I did not feel threatened at all – it seemed gentle.

Once I opened up to the presence I had a strong feeling of recognition. I knew that this invisible presence that was in my bedroom was raspberry. How did I know this? Because since I was tiny I had spent a lot of time with raspberry canes in the garden, and now as an adult I had a field of raspberry canes that my partner and I had planted. I knew in the same way that you can sometimes sense when a friend is already waiting for you in the cafe where you are meeting as you walk through the door. In the same way that you know if your partner has silently walked into the room and is watching you, even before they speak.

I knew it was raspberry because my energy field or being has become attuned to the vibration of this plant and I feel familiar with it. This is why hanging out with plants and spending time with them in their habitat is crucial to getting to know them on a deeper level and really become attuned to them. This connection goes way beyond our knowledge of their appearance, growing habits, fragrance, taste or medicinal properties; it's an alignment with their energetic vibration and essence. As discussed earlier, we are nature too, and we are already attuned to the language or vibration of nature consciousness, so the more time we spend using our hearts as the primary organ of perception and recalibrating our vibration to that of the nature around us, the easier it is to understand it and to remember this common language that we share.

So, to finish the raspberry story, what does one do when woken by it in the night? I opened up to the presence or vibration of raspberry in the room. I couldn't see anything; it was pitch black – there certainly wasn't a beautiful red raspberry deva standing in front of me with her hands on her hips or anything like that, though I do love that image! I just quietly focused on my heart, opened up all of my senses and listened. No voice called out to me in the darkness or whispered in my ear. There was no sound; I felt the vibration of the meaning of the words through my body. A sense that I was not even really aware of before the experience took over and I felt the sense of what raspberry was trying to communicate. Which was that the plants were feeling totally neglected.

Oops. Once the thought of raspberry feeling neglected popped into my mind, I dropped into my heart again and silently asked the question to confirm my suspicion. There was a distinct vibration of agreement, a yes. Oops again! Again silently, I apologized and vowed to rectify this the following day. My response was obviously satisfactory because the presence departed, leaving me a little stunned but awake enough to note it down before drifting off to sleep again.

It was true; the raspberry plants had been a bit neglected over the season. The next morning I reflected on this nocturnal visitation and thought about them. I had not paid them a visit for some time, since the deer ate all their flowering tops. We had been very disappointed that there would be no berries and had not thought to give the plants any specific attention. Later that day I visited the raspberries with an offering of wine and tobacco to thank them for their growth on our land, and it felt like raspberry had heard me.

Reflecting on this event now, I realize raspberry must have been pretty darn desperate to pay me a night-time visit with this request. Perhaps the plants had tried on numerous occasions to get my attention and I was just too busy in my mental space to notice. Maybe raspberry chose to visit me at night because being asleep in the dream state was the only time when my mind was at rest or at peace enough for the plants to get their voices heard. Whatever the reason, this is a pattern for me; it all kicks off for me when the lights go down.

We are all, though, particularly receptive to messages from our unconscious mind during the periods in between sleep and waking. Pay attention to these times at night and try 'lying in wait' for messages and guidance to appear.

Hearing Voices

When I was visited in the night by spruce, the experience was not at all subtle! One night as I was enjoying some much-needed sleep, a message leapt out from the darkness and awakened me.

I clearly heard the words 'It doesn't have to be beeswax.' I don't remember now whether the voice was male or female; or maybe it didn't register because I was too busy being surprised and begrudgingly making myself pay attention.

'Err, okay,' I heard myself saying in my mind's eye. I turned over and scribbled a note in the pad beside my bed – remembering every instance like this is often not possible and a written record helps put my mind at rest. I resumed my sleep.

A few days later I was attending a women's drumming circle and sweat lodge; there had recently been a ritual and celebration on and for a new piece of community shared land, so we were feeling into that energy. Among the offerings that were given as part of the ceremony were many seeds that were blessed, offered and sprinkled about the land. In the centre of our circle were a small handful of those seeds, and my friend who was holding the circle suggested that we create some sort of object using the seeds pressed into something, like beeswax, which could be worn or carried as a symbol of the community energy that holds the shared land.

An excited voice leapt out of me: 'It doesn't have to be beeswax!'

I explained to the group about the message that I had received and, although I do not know what the alternative to beeswax might be, the seeds were handed over to me and along with them the job of creating this symbol.

I pondered this for a week or so. 'If it's not beeswax that holds the seeds together, then what is it to be?' I would ask.

My answer became clear one morning as I was walking my dogs along our lane. There had been a recent storm, which had ravaged some of the trees. In front of me was a beautiful spruce with a branch that had been ripped off and was weeping resin. Excitedly I collected the resin, thanking the tree, and took it home to melt it down. I pressed the seeds into it, with a ribbon so that the token could be worn like a pendant around the neck.

This is a great example of not only hearing a voice but acting on it and honouring the information. I could have simply shrugged off the message, not written it down and forgotten about it; but fortunately I was able to act on the information because my pace of life and receptivity meant that I was not only sensitive to this kind of vibration but in an environment that allowed me the time and space to act on it.

Often we ignore the subtle messages of the spirit world because our beautiful egos enjoy the high stress and drama of our modern life and fool us into thinking that subtle messages aren't important and we don't have enough time for them. How many times have you fooled yourself into thinking that you would remember a dream because it was so vivid when you woke up, but failed to note it down and then realized that by breakfast the memory had faded?

In my experience, the universe always responds in kind to our actions, so the more we can slow down and feel with our hearts, the more we open up to the vibration of the subtle spirit realm and the more we will find ourselves guided when we allow ourselves the space in which to cultivate this sanctuary.

Talking to a Plant

Sit with a plant with whom you are already well acquainted. Try asking the plant some questions (I give some suggestions in the exercise below); go slowly and after asking each question sit and breathe, focusing on your heart centre, and wait for any sort of response. You can ask the plant the questions by speaking out loud or simply holding the question in your heart. Remember, the plant's way of communicating may not be in words; it might come in the form of a thought, memory, a bodily sensation, feeling, colour or something entirely else. Just be open to all the ways in which the plant may respond to you. Be patient, remain free of judgement and be kind to yourself. Expect to be affected emotionally; this is the primary language of plants.

When I first started to do this, I used to imagine that I was at a party and I was meeting someone new. In my imagination I would hold the image of myself sitting alone on a huge white sofa waiting for the arrival of my new friend, the plant I was about to meet. I would hold this image in my imagination while I sat with the plant inviting it to communicate with me. Try using this visualization if it sounds appealing.

I often burst into tears when I am communicating with plants in this way and this is a great gauge for me – if the plant's response touches me emotionally then I know I have asked the right question and I must listen and feel deeply for the answer.

Consider carefully the questions that you will ask. We live in an age where information is so easy to obtain; we can find data on almost anything, to the point where information may sometimes become devalued. Think carefully about the questions for your plant. What are you going to do with the answers? What information do you really need right now and how are you going to act on it? Try not to make your questions idle ones.

Remember that we are a small part of a much greater whole, so you can think cosmically when communicating with plants. Consider asking for wisdom that is not solely for your personal benefit but for that of the wider community. Remember to offer your services to the plant and find out what you can offer the plant.

EXERCISE Deep Listening

Focus on your heart centre, pray for understanding and choose a question to ask the plant. Consider these:

- What is your name/what may I call you?
- Why are you growing here?
- Do you like growing here?
- What can you tell me about this area?
- What can you see?
- Do you have a special role here?
- What can you tell me about plants like yourself?
- Can you show me what you know about well-being?
- Please can you share your wisdom with me in a way that I will understand?
- How can this medicine help?
- Please show me how to nourish… (a plant or a project).
- What is your truth?
- Do you have a dream?
- What are you needs?/How can I help you?

Sense into the plant; does it need anything from you? Will it help you with your healing journey? Does it need to be with you physically? Do you need to make this plant into a medicine or carry it about your person?

- As you sit and breathe, asking questions, notice where your mind goes and bring it gently back.
- Give thanks appropriately to the plant and leave the area.
- Did anything surprise or disappoint you about the response you received?

Note your observations in your journal. See if you are guided to specific books to look up any further information about the plant and be vigilant to any other information in the form of dreams or signs in nature that may be carrying the answers to your questions.

It can be a challenge to trust your own inspiration and observations when working with plants. Obviously it is important to learn about their known uses, traditional and modern, to get as wide a background as possible. However, that knowledge combined with your experience of being with your green allies can give rise to whole new levels of understanding, which can be transformational. So be open and allow that to happen.

Dowsing for Energy and Answers

Dowsing works by tapping into the electromagnetic field given off by everything. It is traditionally associated with searching for underground water, but these days dowsing is also used in healing, earth energies, archaeology and even to find missing people.

This fascinating skill takes practice and patience, but if you are interested in asking specific questions to a plant then you can give it a go.

You can easily pick up a crystal pendulum, a pair of L-shaped rods or a V-rod through crystal suppliers or online. If you want to create your own, a pendulum is easily made using a chain with an object, like a ring, hanging on it. If you are particularly sensitive and put in the practice, you may find that you don't even need a pendulum but that your body will act as your antennae.

Dowsing requires the use of very specific questions rather than open-ended ones, as well as daily practice until your results become consistent. Experiment by using dowsing to choose or place plants in your garden; you can ask about the viability of seeds, when to sow and where to plant out. You can also ask plants specific questions, like those outlined in the exercise above, about their wisdom and how they can help you with healing. The better your questions, the more accurate the results of your dowsing will become.

EXERCISE **Talking to a Tree**

I find it really useful sometimes when out in nature to offload my thoughts and feelings to a nearby (and willing!) tree. I suppose you might say that in this scenario I am talking at a plant rather than having a two-way conversation, but it feels like it works well. In my experience trees do not seem to mind as long as they are treated with respect and kindness. Trees are excellent at holding space for us; they are heaven and earth in one with their roots connected deep and wide into the earth and their branches reaching up to the heavens. I often feel as though I am connecting to the wisdom of the ancestors as I lean in and tell my story to a tree.

If you have something on your mind, get out in nature and use your peripheral vision to select a tree to support you. Introduce yourself to it and breathe together for a few minutes. When you feel ready, ask permission to tell the tree your story and feel into the response. If it feels warm and inviting then go ahead; if not, move on – choose another tree or find another solution.

Ask the tree to witness your feelings, your story and your secrets. I find it useful to express myself fully and out loud to the tree, especially if the issue that is bothering me is frustrating and emotional. It's very cathartic to express myself and feel heard.

Give it a try – tell your story to a tree! You may well find that it ends in a hug. After you have done so, ask yourself, do you feel heard? Feel into the tree. Does it offer you any kind of response or has it just absorbed the energy of your words and your pain or frustration?

As always, give thanks accordingly.

EXERCISE Asking Nature for the Answer

One of my favourite ways of connecting with nature consciousness with a question to solve is to go for a walk, either alone or with my dog.

Next time you have something on your mind, perhaps a decision that you need to make or a solution that you need to find for a problem, take yourself on a walk out to a green space for a minimum of 20 minutes. Hold your question in your heart with an intention to be shown the solution.

While you walk, keep your attention on your heart space and open your eyes, ears and all your other senses, both physical and invisible, to the nature around you. Be open to finding the solution to your challenge – or at the very least a new perspective on it – while you walk.

After your walk check in with yourself and see how you feel now. Has anything shifted? How does your problem look now?

EXERCISE Plants as Mirrors

Each plant that we connect with deeply reflects a part of us and helps us in the process of remembering and bringing ourselves back to a place of wholeness.

Have you ever felt like a plant is mirroring an aspect of yourself or your life?

Sometimes as you walk in the area close to your home you may notice a new plant growing or one that you have not really paid attention to before now. Consider whether this may warrant further investigation to help you with a current challenge.

Alternatively, take a walk in nature with the intention of finding a plant that represents a certain person in your life. See what calls to you. Get closer, observe, breathe together and make friends. How does this plant reflect back to you this person and your relationship? What can you learn and take away from this experience?

Questions for Self-reflection

1. What insights have you gained so far? And how can you act on these?
2. If you have started to note down your dreams, what do you notice?
3. Have you found a plant that matches your personality, or can help with a personal challenge or health issue that you currently face?
4. How can you explore your plant interactions further?

Chapter Summary

With your body, eyes, ears and heart ready to receive and attuned to the subtle language of nature, there are many ways to experience the wisdom teachings of plants.

KEY POINTS

- Note down your dreams and ask for guidance before you sleep.
- Slow down so you can cultivate space and time to receive the blessings of nature and respond to any guidance, inspiration or wisdom that you receive from plants.
- Converse with plants in a way that feels right for you.
- Carefully consider what questions you are asking and always act on the responses.

In the final chapter we consider what all this is for. What can you do with this wisdom and connection? What purpose can your deepening relationship with the plant kingdom serve?

The Power Is You

We are activating the codes for all the Sacred Keepers
You are the Sacred Keepers
We are the Sacred Keepers
Keepers of the Sun
Keepers of the Earth Wisdom
Keepers of the light
Keepers of the sacred love joining
Living in the light, living in the right,
Being on the Earth,
Earth living from the Earth,
Earth giving for the Earth,
Earth returning light, Light becoming Earth.
Regenerating, re-energizing, a new generation from the last
Old in the new, holding the new,
Now.

— May 2017, Queen's Crescent Gardens, Glasgow

I believe that as we attune to the plants and other living elements of our environment and interact more consciously, we begin to grasp a greater sense of our power and identity as a creature of this earth. Now that you have a more intimate relationship with the plants that grow around you, can you recognize the potential and value of a partnership with the spirit of plants? My hope is that you have been touched by the plants in a way that is magical and meaningful for you, as the vital force of plants connects to the vital force within you.

If you feel that you have come to a deeper level of understanding of the green kingdom and a stronger relationship with nature, what is opening for you? Keep following the flow to maintain the open channels of communication. Explore like a child this new friendship, keep questioning, keep listening, keep those plants in your heart. In my experience, as we attune to plants life becomes more dynamic and meaningful.

After practising many of the sensory exercises, you will have hopefully 'Come to your Senses' and have more experience of what your special senses are and how you receive communication from plants. You will also have more self-awareness and familiarity with your heart space and a deepening of the place of knowing that is within you.

What is it that you need to support your self-awareness?

How can you continue to cultivate this space of knowing?

Celebrate Your Connections
Large and Small

By spending time purposefully feeling into plant consciousness and honouring nature from your heart space, you will form strong and intimate bonds with plants. You may have identified one particular plant ally to support you with a current challenge that you face; or have found a special place in nature that resonates with you and fills you with joy and peace. Once recognized, the green world will find a way to weave itself into every aspect of your life. Some of these interactions are so subtle that, amidst the general onslaught of busyness that we face today, it's easy to miss them or take them for granted. However, it's vital that you maintain your mindset of honouring and appreciation. When you are fortunate enough to interact with a plant that becomes your ally and shares its wisdom teachings with you, you should use this information, act on it wisely and share appropriately. If you don't act on it, the medicine becomes like a gift that was unwanted and stayed unopened. Likewise if you don't nurture your relationships with plants, continue to honour, communicate and give thanks, then you may find the relationships fade and are not as potent as they once were.

Making sure that time outside every day, with your heart and senses open, is part of your routine is a good way to maintain your connection to nature. Greeting the day with a smile and a silent thank you, noticing a tree, slowing down to simply look around you for things that are green and growing are all ways to honour and consciously interact with the living elements of your environment. What I'm really saying is 'Take time to smell the roses'!

Weave plants into everyday occasions – grow herbs, cook with fresh organic ingredients, buy flowers, appreciate green spaces, marvel at how tall trees can grow, buy from sustainable sources, find herbal alternatives to your everyday ailments, include plant prayers in your daily ritual, water those office plants, walk in the rain, soak up the sun, escape to the outdoors whenever you can. Simpler still is to pause as you reach for your morning cuppa and silently acknowledge that this daily essential, whether it's tea or coffee, is an interaction with a plant. Find friends and like-minded plant people to share your experiences with and to join you in celebrating the seasons of the year.

As you connect more deeply and embrace the natural world with your heart, it's not unusual to feel sadness at the suffering of the earth and its destruction at our hands. Have faith and be tender with yourself. Your actions of blessing, honouring and interacting consciously with plants will not go unnoticed and are just as important as switching to a more environmentally friendly way of life.

Questions for Self-reflection

1. Looking back at your notes from the start of this plant journey at the beginning of the book, has anything changed?
2. How are you feeling now towards plants and the environment where you live?
3. What insights have you gained?
4. How can you deepen your own self-care, understanding and plant relationships?
5. How can you further work with the plant that chose you? What can you co-create?
6. If you don't feel that connecting to the spirit of plants, in the ways outlined in this book, is for you then what would feel of value? Is it important to you to consider how we cultivate, harvest and use plants? If not, what has more meaning for you? What role do plants play for you in your life?

Inspired Action

I believe that, as we creatures of the earth heal, our journey to health and harmony also heals the earth. Connecting with plants is a dance. It is a journey towards restoring wholeness. Your story, like mine, may be a slow unfolding discovery; it may be an opening that you leap through with bravado or creep through tentatively, feeling your way along, trying to piece all the clues together. Each interaction, acknowledgement or honouring helps restore the relationship between humans and plants more broadly; as you are touched by the spirit of plants, so too are many others. How does this relationship with and respect for nature fit into your life and the world in general? What are you inspired or guided to co-create with nature?

Are you inspired to grow plants? Volunteer in your community garden? Start a movement? Paint or create with nature? Make plant medicines? Use natural products?

The Dream of the Earth – What Role Can You Play?

Imagine that deep within the centre of the earth lies the earth heart, pulsating, creating and dreaming into being every wonder that exists on earth. A vibrant and ancient symphony of green and gold, spinning our world from her dreamtime into our reality.

I'm fascinated by imagining what the dream of the earth and her plants and creatures could be. I wonder how we fit into the dream at the heart of the earth; are we a burden? Do we disappoint? Are we ruining her dream or are we just an amusement? Does the earth feel down, like we do when our dreams don't seem to be coming to fruition? Through this meditation below I invite you to journey into the heart of the earth and experience the story to be found there and the part that will be revealed to you. In this way perhaps you will be inspired to align your actions towards helping the dream of the earth's heart come true.

If you don't wish to do the meditation, you can instead simply sit, breathe and ask a favourite plant who you resonate with: 'What can I do? Will you show me my role?'

MEDITATION Connect with the Earth Heart

Sit quietly where you will not be disturbed. If you can be warm and comfortable outside then sit outside; otherwise remain indoors.

Close your eyes to help yourself turn inwards. Focus your attention on your breath. Making your exhalation long and purposeful, breathe into the depths of your body. Be in this moment, leaving the cares and concerns of your ordinary life aside.

Become aware of your body as you breathe and mindfully sweep your attention over your body, lovingly noticing any areas of discomfort, pain or tension. Send your breath there and pause for a while over each area, relaxing a little more with each exhalation.

Focus now on your heart centre as you breathe, as if breathing from the heart. Send your breath there when you inhale and imagine as you exhale that the heart itself is breathing out. Allow the heart area to soften and slowly, like a flower unfolding, allow your petals to open. Stay breathing here like this and feel compassion for yourself, as if each breath in is filling you with love and each breath out is sending love out to the world.

Imagine that roots are sprouting from your feet; watch how these roots flow down and anchor you to the earth. Follow these strong roots as they travel deep down into the earth. Travelling through all of the strata, all of the layers of the earth, through nutritious rich topsoil, layers of granite, schist, sand, ancient decomposing matter, crystals, gemstones, travelling deep down towards the heart of the earth. Sense the pull of these roots as they gently but firmly hold you to the earth. Notice also, as the roots are travelling down, that there are many other roots of other beings also heading straight for the centre of the earth.

As you get a sense of reaching the centre, feel the warmth radiating from this molten core. Sense your roots dipping into a warm green gold liquid, the sweet nectar of creation.

Sense your roots drinking this nectar and nourishment up and bringing this sustenance all the way up and up and up your roots, up through the earth's layers into your feet. Feel this warm golden liquid spreading from your feet all the way through your body, touching every organ, bone, muscle, blood vessel, filling your body with golden nectar of the earth. Feel this nectar pool as a golden glowing light at your heart centre. Your heart centre is now linked with the heart centre of the earth.

Breathe here in this space, breathe into your heart centre and sense yourself rooted firmly to the earth, joined to her, fed by the earth, receiving nourishment and love through your roots. See if you can really get a sense of this link that binds you.

If there are areas of your body that you feel need more nourishment or soothing than others, ask that the golden nectar go there specifically and visualize the golden glow surrounding the parts of your body that need it most, feeling loved, nourished, soothed and calm.

Now turn your focus to your heart and as you breathe into this green/golden space in which you are connected to the centre of the earth, allow your heart to open just a little bit more, opening up to the golden sustenance of the earth, opening up to her nourishment and support. Breathe with your focus on your heart, allowing the golden glow in, softening, receiving.

Turn your inner attention now to the heavens; imagine a big diamond light radiating the magical colours of the universe is shining down onto you. Sense this diamond light reaching you and, from the divine, entering through the crown of your head. Feel the sense of magical power and beauty that this magnificent light carries. Allow this light into your body, so it lights up first your head, neck, shoulders and arms; then sweeps down through your heart, through all of your major organs, into your digestive system, your pelvic region and down your legs to your feet. Breathe and absorb this divine light, feeling the glow of love and infinite possibility that shines on you from the angelic realms of the divine.

Bathe in the glory of this diamond light and allow it to mingle with the golden glow that is already filling you with nourishment from the earth. Focus on your heart as the centre of where these two loving sources meet and mingle within you. Golden sustenance, creative force and nourishment from the earth, diamond light of love, magic and infinite possibility from the heavens. Feel the brilliance of heaven and earth joining in you. Bask in the glow. Drink up the power of the two energies.

From your heart, focusing on the diamond light, send the light down through your body to your feet. Imagine the light flowing from the top of your crown through your body, down to your feet and beyond you, into the earth. Sense this diamond light of infinite possibility and love flowing down into the earth, following your roots, flowing down, down, down through the different layers of the earth. Down into the heart of the earth.

Feel the flow of this divine light, coming now right down from the heavens, in through your crown, through your heart, flowing through the rest of your body, down through the soles of your feet and into the earth. Flowing and shining its diamond light through your roots into the centre of the earth. Filling the centre of the earth with light and love from the divine, flooding the centre of the earth with love and the diamond light of infinite possibility and magic. Sense this flow, breathe in this wonderful connection that is made possible by you. By your willingness to receive energy from the earth and the heavens, you join earth and the heavens and the earth heart is able to receive divine love and light. Breathe here, sensing the flow down from the heavens. Notice any sensations that you are feeling in your body, relax and breathe.

Bring your focus back to your body and visualize a hole appearing in the ground next to you. A staircase appears in the hole, inviting you down to visit the earth heart.

In ten steps you are going to reach the earth heart.

Ten, nine, eight, seven, six, five, four, three, two and one.

You now find yourself in a large cave at the centre of the earth. Look around you at where you have landed. There is a golden glow up ahead; move closer to the golden glow.

As you approach the glow, you start to feel warm and almost blinded by this golden-green light that is coming from the centre of the earth. Visualize this however it naturally comes to you; you may see pools of bubbling warm golden-green nectar, a glowing crystal cave, a bubbling cauldron or a golden cloud of energy. How does this heart centre show itself to you?

When the time feels right, enter into the heart of this golden glow. This may mean you have to enter the golden pool, or cloud of energy, or simply touch a golden crystal in front of you.

Make this connection with the heart centre now.

Send the heart centre all of your love and gratitude for the creation that you experience here on earth. Wait for the heart to receive.

Hold in your heart the intention to befriend the earth, get to know her better – you mean her no harm, you want to be friends. Hold in your heart the intention that you wish to help the earth if you can.

Sit breathing in the golden glow of the earth at her centre. Notice any sensations that enter your body, or any emotions that come up for you. Sit, breathe, sensing, feeling... Send your love to the earth, listen and wait for the earth to receive.

Spend as long as you need to connect deeply with the earth heart. If you are able to make a strong connection then ask the earth to show you her story, and pay attention to what you receive.

Ask to be shown your role here on earth and what you can do to help. Allow yourself to relax and receive.

When you feel ready to leave give your thanks to the earth and know that you can return to this place at any time.

Return the way you came through the cave and when you reach the steps start climbing, knowing that when you reach the top you will be back on the earth. Start climbing now:

One, two, three, four, five, six, seven, eight, nine and ten. Now you are back on the surface of the earth, where you live. See the entrance to the steps closing but know that you can go back and summon them at any time.

Now focus back into your heart. You are still connected to the diamond light of the divine and the golden glow of the earth; sense the flow of them both through your body. You are going to carry this connection with you as you awaken.

Enjoy a few final slow breaths here and then begin to become more aware of your body; start to move your fingers and toes, wrists and ankles. When you are ready open your eyes.

Take out your notebook and as soon as you can, note down anything that you have experienced. Even if something doesn't seem directly relevant, note it down.

Listen to the meditation at **www.plantsthatspeak.com**.

Together let's start listening to what the earth has to tell us. Let's discover what story the earth and her plants have to share. Let's be brave and discover what role we can play in the earth's big dream. Let's be conscious of our connection to the earth, her plants and creatures; let's sense into this whenever we can, making choices and taking actions that feel aligned with this co-creative relationship.

Let's endeavour each day to honour the dream of the earth. Let's be sure that we know what our dream is and hold the vision.

If this book has touched your life in any way then take your gratitude and blessings to the plants. These words and insights have come through me, my teachers and students following all our encounters with the green kingdom over the past seven years or more.

May you continue to discover more about the plants that grow in your local area and how you can work together to improve your life and the lives of those around you. Keep opening, keep expanding your heart space and consciousness until you find your plant allies and form deep and transformational relationships. This heart-centred journey for you, this dance with the green kingdom does not have an end. Your plant friends will be your allies and lead you to health, understanding and happiness if you continue to honour them and treat them with respect. Who knows what they really can offer us and what secrets and wisdom they have to share? We haven't even really begun to discover the depths of what lies waiting for us in the green embrace of our plant friends. Our role is to unfold, explore and feel our way back into their embrace as we journey towards wholeness. Travel further, explore deeper and discover the magic of who you really are.

Chapter Summary

Our journey together has come to an end but don't let your adventure with the spirit of nature finish here. Let it unfold and flow with the seasons, dance in the wind and open like a flower in the sun. Feel your way back to harmony, not just with the green spaces and plant allies that surround you, but back to a deeper and more authentic connection with others and your true sense of self.

KEY POINTS

- Weave plants into your everyday and celebrate this connection: 'take time to smell the roses' (while they are still here!).
- Strengthen what has meaning for you and develop key (plant) relationships.
- Stay conscious of your connection to the earth, her plants and creatures and play your role in the story of the earth heart.

Acknowledgements

Grateful thanks go to everyone who helped make this book become a reality. Many thanks to everyone who has ever participated with me in a workshop and the teachers, healers, herbalists and shamanic practitioners who have held space for me to participate, transform and commune with plants and spirit. My heart shines brightly with gratitude to all those brothers and sisters who have sat with me in sacred circles to witness my truth and power. Humble thanks to all of the plants, herbal healers and plant teachers who have crossed my path with so many blessings and teachings to enrich my journey and share with others. Thanks to Findhorn Press for recognizing this project as one of their own. Finally, heartfelt thanks to my wonderful partner Jamie for always supporting me, keeping my passion alive and walking by my side throughout all the adventures.

Appendix

Plant Connection Checklist

Preparation

1. Check your attitude and actions: are you making conscious choices to help the environment and meet the plant as a friend? How do you show your gratitude and honour the plants you live with appropriately? What is your true motivation for connecting with plants?
2. Heart Space not Head Space: drop your awareness down from your head (mental space) into your heart apace. See, feel and experience through the heart.

Interacting with Plants and Nature

3. Awareness and Flow: be mindful of your feelings, how you feel in your physical body and what is going on for you mentally, emotionally and spiritually. Be conscious of the state of flow in your life. What is flowing? What is not flowing? What feels right to flow with? What feels right to stop?
4. Peripheral Vision: use your peripheral vision to notice which plants wish to work with you and help you. Allow a plant to choose you.

Meeting a Plant

5. First Impressions: how does the plant touch you? Note and observe your feelings, thoughts, memories, physical sensations and visuals.
6. Introduce yourself and start up conversation: tell the plant your name and your story.
7. Open your Senses: sit by the plant, breathe and observe: How does the plant make you feel? Really spend time watching how the plant grows and observing each and every characteristic. If it feels right touch, smell, listen to and taste the plant.

8. Take time to breathe: spend time breathing with the plant, offering your breath and receiving the plant's oxygen.

9. Open your heart and RECEIVE: be still, listen, sense the plant and feel into the space between you. Place the plant into your heart. How does the plant feel? Notice sensations in your body, colours, emotions, thoughts and memories.

10. Offerings and giving thanks: show your gratitude for the plant's willingness to work with you. Compliment the plant; be gentle and kind. Give an appropriate offering.

Follow-up and Inspired Action

11. Integration, Action and Honouring: take time to absorb your time with the plant and let the energy settle. How can you honour the teachings of the plant? What wisdom teachings does it hold for you? How can you best absorb these? Get creative: poetry, dance, song, painting, ceremony, elixir-making… Notice your dreams and other synchronicities; note your thoughts and feelings.

12. Maintain Your Relationship and Keep Following the Flow: keep the plant in your awareness, feeling into your intuition about what is needed.

Plant Observation Sheet	
Plant Name	General Observations
Plant size (absolute, and also in relation to others growing nearby) and form	
Location: e.g., sun/shade, type of area/soil	
Location in relation to other plants or animals	
Is the plant isolated or are there others of the same species nearby?	
What does the area where the plant is growing feel like?	
Stage of growth: i.e., in bud/flower/ seed – is this in keeping with other plants in the area?	
How is the plant growing?– spreading/upright/twisted/cramped	
General appearance: e.g., healthy/ bug-eaten, happy/strong/weak?	
What attracted you to the plant?	

Plant Observation Sheet	
Plant Name	**General Observations**
Favourite feature of the plant and reasons why	
What is the first thought that comes into your mind when you see this plant (your first impression)?	
If the plant was trying to tell you something what might it say?	
Does the plant seem friendly?	
How do you feel about the plant? Where do you feel this in your body?	
What part of the body/mind or which ailment do you feel this plant has an affinity for?	
Colour – does this plant have a special colour or bring to mind any colours or patterns?	
Without touching it, how does it look like it will feel?	
Other sensations/feelings/ observations/patterns	

Index of Practices

Bibliography

Bartram, Thomas. *Encyclopedia of Herbal Medicine*. Dorset, UK: Ashgrove Press, 1995.

Brown, Elizabeth. *Dowsing: The Ultimate Guide for the 21st Century*. London: Hay House UK, 2010.

Buhner, Stephen Harrod. *Sacred Plant Medicine: The Wisdom in Native American Herbalism*. Rochester, Vt.: Bear & Co., 2006.

_____. *The Lost Language of Plants. The Ecological Importance of Plant Medicines to Life on Earth*. White River Junction, Vt.: Chelsea Green, 2000.

Carr-Gomm, Phillip, and Stephanie Carr-Gomm. *The Druid Plant Oracle*. London: Connections, 2007.

Coelho, Paulo. *The Warrior of the Light*. London: Harper, 2011.

Coleridge, Samuel Taylor and Wordsworth, William. *Lyrical Ballads 1798 – 1802*. Oxford,UK: Oxford Press, 2013.

Colquhoun, Margaret and Ewald, Axel. *New Eyes for Plants: A Workbook for Plant Observation and Drawing*. Stroud, UK: Hawthorn Press, 1996.

Conway, Peter. *Tree Medicine*. London: Piatkus, 2001.

Cowan, Eliot. *Plant Spirit Medicine: A Journey into the Healing Wisdom of Plants*. Boulder, CO.: Sounds True Inc., 2014.

Cruden, Loren. *Medicine Grove: A Shamanic Herbal*. Rochester, Vt.: Destiny Books, 1997.

Culpeper, Nicholas. *Culpeper's Complete Herbal and English Physician*. London, UK: Harvery Sales, 1981.

Cunningham, Scott. *Cunningham's Encyclopedia of Magical Herbs*. Woodbury, Minn.: Llewellyn, 1985.

Dahl, Roald. *The Minpins*. London: Puffin, 2013.

Elpel, Thomas. *Botany in a Day: Thomas J. Elpel's Herbal Field Guide to Plant Families*. Pony, MT.: HOPS Press, 2008.

Findhorn Community. *The Findhorn Garden*. Forres, UK: Findhorn Press, 1975.

Foster, Steven and Duke, James, A. *Peterson Field Guide to Medicinal Plants and Herbs of Eastern and Central North America, Third Edition (Peterson Field Guides)* Boston, MA.: Houghton Mifflin, 2014.

Fukuoka, Masanobu. *The Natural Way of Farming*. Madras, India: Book Venture, 1993.

Giono, Jean. *The Man Who Planted Trees*. London: Peter Owen Ltd, 2008.

Green, James. *The Herbal Medicine-Maker's Handbook*: A Home Manual. New York: Crossing Press, 2000.

Grieve, Maude. *A Modern Herbal*. London: Penguin, 1980.

Griggs, Barbara. *The Green Witch: A Modern Woman's Herbal*. London: Vermillion Books, 1993.

Guyett, Carole. *Sacred Plant Initiations*. Rochester, Vt.: Bear & Co., 2015.

Harner, Michael. *The Way of the Shaman*. New York: HarperCollins Publishers, 1990.

Heaven, Ross, and Charing, Howard. *Plant Spirit Shamanism*. Rochester, Vt.: Destiny Books, 2006.

Hoffman, David. *The Holistic Herbal: A Herbal Celebrating the Wholeness of Life*. Forres, UK: Findhorn Press, 1983.

Hopman, Ellen Evert. *A Druid's Herbal for the Sacred Earth Year*. Rochester, Vt.: Destiny Books, 1995.

Hughes, Marilynn. *World Religions and their Prophets*. The Out-of-Body Travel Foundation, 2006.

Ingerman, Sandra. *Soul Retrieval*. New York: Harper Collins Publishers, 1991.

_____. *Medicine for the Earth: How to Transform Personal and Environmental Toxins*. New York: Three Rivers Press, 2000.

_____. *Walking in Light: The Everyday Empowerment of a Shamanic Life*. Boulder, CO. Sounds True Inc., 2015.

Ingerman, Sandra and Roberts, Llyn. *Speaking with Nature*. Rochester, Vt.: Bear & Co., 2015.

Kindred, Glennie. *Sacred Celebrations: A Sourcebook*. Glastonbury: Gothic Image Publications, 2001.

_____. *The Sacred Tree*. Matlock, UK: Glennie Kindred, 2003.

Kollerstrom, Nick. *Gardening and Planting by the Moon 2017*. Slough, UK: W. Foulsham & Co. Ltd., 2016.

Linn, Denise. *Sacred Space: Clearing and Enhancing the Energy of your Home*. New York: Ballantine, 1995.

McIntyre, Anne. *Flower Power*. New York: Henry Holt & Co., 1996.

_____. *The Complete Woman's Herbal*. London: Gaia Books Ltd, 1994.

MacCaskill, Don. *Listen To The Trees*. Edinburgh: Luath Press Ltd, 1999.

Martynoga, Fi and Chapman, Emma. *A Handbook of Scotland's Wild Harvests*. Salford, UK: Saraband, 2012.

Matthews, Caitlin. *Singing the Soul Back Home: Shamanic Wisdom for Every Day*. London: Connections Book Publishing, 2002.

Mességué, Maurice. *Health Secrets of Plants and Herbs*. Glasgow: William Collins, 1979.

Montgomery, Pam. *Plant Spirit Healing: A Guide to Working with Plant Consciousness*. Rochester, Vt.: Bear & Co., 2008.

Moss, Robert. *Conscious Dreaming: A Unique Nine-Step Approach to Understanding Dreams*. London: Rider Books, 2014.

Muir, John. *John of the Mountains: The unpublished Journals of John Muir*. Madison: University of Wisconsin Press, 1979.

Narby, Jeremy. *Intelligence in Nature*. New York: Penguin Group Inc., 2005.

Paterson, Jacqueline Memory. *Tree Wisdom: The Definitive Guidebook to the Myth, Folklore and Healing Power of Trees*. London: Thorsons, 1996.

Prechtel, Martin. *Secrets of the Talking Jaguar*. New York: Jeremy P. Tarcher/ Putnam, 1998.

Scott, Michael. *Scottish Wild Flowers*. London: HarperCollins Publishers Ltd., 2008.

Selhub, Eva M. and Logan, Alan C. *Your Brain on Nature: The Science of Nature's Influence on Your Health, Happiness and Vitality*. London: Collins Publishers, 2014.

Small Wright, Machaelle. *Perelandra Garden Workbook: A Complete Guide to Gardening with Nature Intelligence*. Warrenton, VA.: Perelandra, 1993.

Starhawk. *The Earth Path: Grounding Your Spirit in the Rhythms of Nature*. New York: HarperOne, 2006.

Sterry, Paul. *Collins Complete Guide to British Trees: A Photographic Guide to Every Common Species*. London: HarperCollins Publishers Ltd., 2008.

_____. *British Wild Flowers: A Photographic Guide to Every Common Species*. London: HarperCollins Publishers Ltd., 2008.

Tompkins, Peter and Bird, Christopher. *The Secret Life of Plants*. New York: Avon Books, 1973.

Villoldo, Alberto. *Shaman, Healer, Sage*. New York: Harmony Books, 2000.

Weed, Susun. *Healing Wise*. Woodstock, N.Y.: Ash Tree Publishing, 1989.

Weeks, Nora and Bullen, Victor. *The Bach Flower Remedies: Illustrations and Preparations*. Essex, UK: CW Daniel Company Ltd., 1990.

About the Author

FAY JOHNSTONE established and developed a flower and herb farm in Nova Scotia, reconnecting with nature and rewilding her inner self. Drawing on this experience as well as her shamanic training, she now brings the subtle whispers of nature to assist us with our personal transformation. Fay offers workshops educating on plant spirit connection and shamanic treatments across the UK, online and from her home in Scotland. For more info please visit **www.fayjohnstone.com**.

FINDHORN PRESS

Life-Changing Books

Learn more about us and our books at
www.findhornpress.com

For information on the Findhorn Foundation:
www.findhorn.org